A Visitor's Guide to Peml
(Tenby and South Coast E

D0413401

CONTENTS

Complete with Free Road Map of West Dyfed and large indexed Street Plan of Tenby. (Also includes Street Plans of Saundersfoot, Pembroke and Pembroke Dock).

Introduction

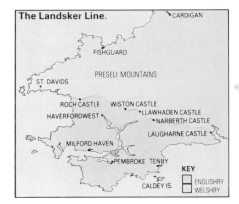

The Landsker Line.

Pembrokeshire affords visitors of all ages and interests a superb opportunity to enjoy a splendidly varied and healthy holiday in unspoilt and picturesque surroundings. Almost all of its spectacular coastline is included in the Pembrokeshire Coast National Park and includes amongst its attractions miles of towering cliffs, with offshore stacks and islands which are justly famous for their colonies of seabirds and profusion of wild flowers. Punctuating these cliffs lie numerous safe, sandy beaches — from small, sheltered rocky coves like Porthmelgan, to the wide expanse of Pendine, some seven miles long. Inland many of the streams and rivers converge and flow into Milford Haven, one of the finest natural harbours in Europe, whose upper reaches of softly wooded creeks and tidal marshes, contrast strongly with the harsh ruggedness of the coastal ramparts.

This fascinating area with its mild climate, clear bright light much beloved by artists and photographers, exhibits its rich, historical background at every turn. The Vikings, Normans and later, Flemings, all influenced the physical and cultural development of South Pembrokeshire. The area contains some of the most impressive castles in Wales — the Normans built a whole series of magnificent fortresses, skilfully positioned for defensive purposes against the hostile Welsh chieftains. The line of castles that includes Roch, Haverfordwest, Wiston, Llawhaden, Narberth and Laugharne formed the main defensive frontier to protect the fertile south — sometimes referred to as "Little England Beyond Wales". This line is the "Landsker Line" and to the North is the Welshry, where the Welsh language dominates and to the South is the Englishry, where very little Welsh is spoken. The Englishry has an important industrial history in the coal and iron industries of Saundersfoot and its hinterland and the shipbuilding activities of Milford Haven. The people of the area are warm and hospitable by nature and fiercely proud of the captivating beauty of this small corner of Wales.

What area is covered by the Guide?

The table of contents reveals a comprehensive attempt to provide the visitor with all the information needed to make his or her holiday in Pembrokeshire as interesting and enjoyable as possible. In particular, the south of the county is covered in special detail. Dealing first with the major holiday centres of Tenby,

Saundersfoot and Pembroke, the Guide then introduces the reader to the three magnificent faces of the Pembrokeshire coastline — the South Coast, the West Coast and the North Coast. Many of the beaches along this exciting coastline are described with the help of a full colour photograph. Next it surveys the creeks, harbours and villages of inland South Pembrokeshire and finally the heather-clad moors and mountain roads of the Preseli Hills where the sheep reigns supreme. Altogether over 130 places of interest to the visitor are presented as only an enthusiastic local author can. Ten car tours, suitable for the whole family, are featured. The guide describes ten of the most enjoyable walks in the south of the county, and has pages packed with information on local sporting and recreational facilities, boat cruises, wildlife parks, museums, gardens to visit, working mills, potteries, etc, etc. It contains a section on evening entertainment, comprehensive suggestions on where to eat and drink, the location of Tourist Information Centres throughout the county and information on essential local holiday services. These features, together with a free Visitor's Road Map to Pembrokeshire and detailed Street Plans combine to make this **the best selling local information Guide in Wales. The four editions published since 1984 have sold nearly 100,000 copies.**

So **WELCOME TO PEMBROKESHIRE.** Keep this guide in your beach bag, or the glove compartment of the car and use it to make the very most of your holiday. But, be warned! "Pembrokeshire-itis" is an acutely infectious condition which can rapidly afflict the unwary tourist, especially those whose senses have been dulled by seasons of packaged holidays in the neon lit, instant concrete resorts of the Costa . . .

. . . Here you will be seduced by the overwhelming natural beauty of coast and countryside, by magnificent limestone castles

Skrinkle Beach near Manorbier.   © *Alan Shepherd Transparency Library.*

steeped in history, by hedgerows and lonely cliff paths full of wild flowers, by islands of timeless tranquility where the grey seal will survey you with a keen eye as he drifts on the ebb and flow of the clear Atlantic surf, and by a quality of life which leaves the rush of the rat race far behind. Unfortunately this condition is progressively addictive, and is only satisfied by further visits of greater length and frequency!

Have a great holiday and come and see us again!

Climate

The peninsular shape of Pembrokeshire, almost bisect by the Milford Haven waterway, ensures the moderating influence of the sea on the climate of the area. The sea influenced by the drift of equatorial water from the Gulf Stream is amongst the warmest in Britain. Winters are mild and coastal frosts infrequent. In the extreme West, Dale and the Castlemartin area have amongst the lowest rainfall figures in Wales, while inland in the more extreme higher altitude conditions of the Preseli Hills, this total exceeds 50 inches. The whole of the Western coastline of

Pembrokeshire has an excellent sunshine record, 1800 hours have been regularly recorded and Dale and Tenby often are the sunniest places in Wales. The region is notoriously windy, however, and the misshapen coastal vegetation reflects the attention of the great winter gales from the Atlantic, (St. Anne's Head is regularly battered by more than 30 major gales each year).

Sea Pinks, Ceibwr Bay, North Pembs.
© *Alan Shepherd Transparency Library.*

3

The Three Main Holiday Centres of South Pembrokeshire

Tenby

"You may travel the world over, but you will find nothing more beautiful: it is so restful, so colourful and so unspoilt." (Augustus John, Artist)

Tenby is the major holiday resort of the area, enjoying a spectacular position astride a small promontary on the Western side of Carmarthen Bay. Its Welsh name Dynbych-y-Pysgod means "Little fort of the fish".

The town is flanked by four magnificent beaches and leads via a network of narrow and picturesque streets and alleys to its original focal point — the small harbour, bustling with brightly painted pleasure boats and sailing craft.

History

After its primitive beginnings as a hill fort, Tenby was frequently visited by the Vikings who are thought to have used the North shore as a base — note the Norse names of "Goscar Rock" (ploughshare), Sker Rock, etc. Later it was captured by the Normans, strongly fortified and used as an important base, together with Pembroke and Haverfordwest, in the Norman colonisation of the South of the County. During this period it was subjected to several furious assaults by the Welsh. In 1153, Maredudd and Rhys, the sons of Gruffydd ap Rhys, attacked the town and slaughtered the garrison of Norman troops. In 1187, Maelgwyn ap Rhys put the small town to the sword and in 1260 it was again sacked, by Prince Llewellyn. It is now believed that many of the streets within the Town Walls date from the reconstruction which followed this last raid. The castle was repaired and the fortifications improved on the orders of Richard III when a French invasion was rumoured in 1377. By now the town had been totally enclosed behind a stout curtain wall which is still in a good state of repair and known as the "Town Walls". In 1402 Henry IV gave the town its first Royal Charter and authorised the election of a

Tenby Harbour and Castle Hill from North Cliff.   © *Alan Shepherd Transparency Library.*

4

Tenby Harbour, showing the old Royal Victoria Pier.

mayor. The entrance hall to Tenby Museum contains a complete list of all the Mayors of Tenby since this date. In 1471, Henry Tudor, (the Earl of Richmond), escaped from Tenby to Brittany in a small sailing ship possibly owned by Thomas White, the then mayor. In 1581, Elizabeth I incorporated Tenby as free borough with its own seal, showing a ship and a castle.

By 1600 the town was one of the principal fortresses and busiest ports in South Wales, (see the Tudor Merchant's House, p.13). Customs records indicate that trade was mainly with West Country ports, Ireland and also with France, Spain and Portugal. Wine and salt were imported and cloth, coal and other merchandise exported. At this time the town was more surrounded by the sea than today. Much of what is Kiln Park Caravan Site today was then part of the marshy tidal estuary of the river Ritec. Sailing ships entered this estuary over a sandy bar, now the Tenby end of the South Beach, to lie at anchor in Holloway's Water, or Pill Lake which lay approximately where the Salterns Trading Estate has now been built (marked on the street plan).

The town displayed erratic loyalties during the civil war with the result that it eventually suffered considerable damage from both sides. It declared for Parliament in 1642, but surrendered to the Royalists in August 1643. In the spring of 1644 it was again recaptured by Colonel Rowland Laugharne for Parliament, after a three-day siege. In 1648 the town joined Mayor Poyer of Pembroke in the South Wales insurrection against Parliament. Cromwell was forced to send a strong force to deal with the revolt and Tenby suffered a damaging three week siege by Colonel Horton, before again surrendering to the Roundheads. One of the articles of this capitulation ran: "That the besieged deliver up all ordnance, arms and ammunition of the castle to Lieutenant-General Cromwell for the use of the Parliament". A military governor was appointed for the remainder of the protectorate and the castle was partially dismantled.

Tenby now entered a period of serious

Sailing Regatta, Tenby Harbour. © A.S.T.L.

social and economic decline. In 1651 the population was decimated by a serious outbreak of Plague, its port trade withered and by the end of the eighteenth century the town was little more than a rather forlorn fishing village, with many of its buildings in semi-ruin. Records indicate that by 1784 so many pigs scavenged around the streets of the town that the town council were eventually forced to appoint two constables to deal with them.

By the latter part of the 18th century, sea resorts were beginning to be established at convivial locations around the coast. Tenby's scenic attractions and clear healthy air began to draw praise and attention. Visiting gentry started to build fine houses during this period, e.g. Sion House, designed by Nash, and built in 1790 (eventually destroyed by fire in 1937), stood on the site now occupied by Croft Court. Croft House, now the Guildhall, was also built at this time. Early in the 19th century the pace of development of the new resorts quickened with changing social conventions. The Prince Regent "took the waters" at Brighton and made the concept of sea bathing fashionable. At the same time, Napoleon was threatening the Continent of Europe and many wealthy visitors were no longer able to travel abroad. In Tenby, Sir William Paxton, a London banker and property owner

North Bay, Tenby, 1817.   *(From a Watercolour by Charles Norris)*

from Carmarthen, was quick to appreciate Tenby's potential as a resort and became the driving force behind the re-development of the town. He lived in Tenby House, Tudor Square from 1805-1824. The town contains many fine examples of Georgian and Victorian architecture, e.g. Croft Terrace (The Croft), built in 1830, St. Julian's Street and Lexden Terrace (1843). Lord Nelson and Lady Hamilton had already visited the town some years earlier and now large numbers began arriving by sea from Bristol (first Steamer 1828) and by horse drawn coaches. A proper piped water supply was installed in 1815 to meet the needs of the growing town, and the filter beds were located where the North Beach Car Park now lies. As the town developed, congestion within the town walls became more severe and residents and visitors were inconvenienced. This led to the Tenby Improvement Act of 1838, after which certain key streets were widened, and offending old buildings were knocked down.

The Railway link with the expanding South Wales rail network was completed in 1866 and this immediately made the town accessible to almost all parts of England and Wales. When the Tenby-Pembroke line crossed the marsh to Penally in 1863, its embankment was built on top of a former embankment, constructed by Sir

John Owen of Orielton as part of an earlier attempt to reclaim the estuary bottom in 1820.

As the number of visitors increased substantially, the town expanded and streets such as Picton Road, Trafalgar Road and Victoria Street were constructed.

The first Guides to the Tenby area were published around 1810 to meet the needs of the new visitors and make fascinating reading, e.g. "A Guide to Tenby and its Neighbourhood" by R. Mason, 1863; "Allen's Tenby", edited by Mrs. F. Gwynne, 1868. The Mason Guide provides details of the corporation bye laws regarding sea bathing: Section 80 indicates that no gentleman's bathing machine must be placed within 50 yards of a lady's machine and that "no boat shall come within 100 yards of any bathing machine when used for bathing". If Victorian visitors wanted to bathe without the aid of a machine they had to do so in a "proper costume' before 8am or after 9pm, except on certain more isolated parts of the beach.

Tenby thus became a popular and fashionable holiday resort, with many fine houses and wealthy residents. Promenading was a popular evening activity and the early guides give details of the most popular areas to promenade. "The Croft Terrace, from its more central position forms perhaps the most fashionable promenade . . . here on band nights stylish visitors parade in piquant and costly costumes, others thronging the seats . . ." This was also the period when making seaside "collections" was very much part of the activities of the well to do visitors, often dried flowers and dried grasses for the ladies and perhaps shells for the gentlemen. The fascinating work by zoologist Philip Gosse, "Tenby: A Seaside Holiday", published in 1856 is a rich source of information on the attitudes and interests of the Victorian visitor. Much stock was placed on long energetic walks to places of interest, and constant reference made to the therapeutic and health giving qualities of sea bathing, the clear Tenby air, and to the mild winter temperatures which "make the resort much suited to over-wintering for invalids".

And so Tenby moved into the 20th century. In 1911, Mrs. Pankhurst visited the town and during the First World War, troops were billeted here. Gradually the rather exclusive nature of the town changed reflecting the changes in society. Advertisements in the local press during the 1920s refer less to the nobility and gentry and more to the needs of the ordinary visitor to the town. Arrangements for swimming also became a little more liberal. In 1932 the Corporation Guide indicates that . . . "the bathing which is permitted by the authorities finds much favour with visitors. They are not compelled to use the machines, but are allowed to bathe at all times from tents, or from the shelter of the cliffs. Mixed bathing has been the rule at Tenby for many years."!!

Between the two world wars, the town expanded in a number of different directions. Houses spread up the Maudlins and Narberth Road, and many of the streets in the area of Park Place, Edward Street, Queen's Parade, etc. were constructed during this period.

After the 1939-45 War Tenby soon realised that its future lay as a popular holiday resort catering for the growing amount of leisure time which the country now began to enjoy. During the 1950's it became a very popular destination for hundreds of week-end motor coach trips from industrial South Wales. From around 1930 the town also received special excursion trains from Swindon for the annual railway works holiday. The later 1950's and 1960's brought the holiday pattern of today with a tremendous growth in the popularity of self catering accommodation of all kinds, mushrooming caravan and tent sites and a mobile population largely travelling in their own cars. The recent introduction of the Inter-City 125 Service, the construction of the M4 motorway and in 1984 the opening of the Kilgetty by-pass and the dual carriageway linking the new road bridge at Carmarthen with St.

Sunday Morning Parade, The Esplanade, Tenby (c.1900)

Tenby Harbour packed with fishing boats, 1875. These three pictures courtesy of Roscoe Howells.

Bathing Machines on the North Sands, Tenby (c. 1890)

South Beach from the Gardens of the Atlantic Hotel.
© Alan Shepherd Transparency Library.

Clears, continue to bring this beautiful resort still closer to the large city conurbations, and assure its immense popularity.

The Beaches

Each of the four fine sandy beaches has its own character, charm and enthusiastic devotees. The well sheltered curve of the **North Beach** nestling under the brown shale cliffs, with the massive landmark of Goscar Rock, is particularly warm and sunny in the morning and early afternoon. **The Harbour Beach** is a much smaller more enclosed beach, ideally placed for watching people "messing about in boats" and the constant busy harbour arrivals and departures. It also has the advantage of full sun all day and late into the evening. **The Castle Beach** faces due South and shelters in the lee of the Castle Hill and St. Catherine's Island. Stretching South Westwards from Castle Beach for 1.5 miles is the broad expanse of the **South Beach** with its superb natural offshore breakwater of Caldey Island and backed for most of its length by sand dunes which afford a natural adventure playground for children.

Swimming is safe from all beaches, particularly the North Beach. Care should be exercised in the vicinity of St. Catherine's Island

because of dangerous currents at certain states of the tide. All beaches have deck chairs and refreshments with toilets nearby. North and South Beaches have nearby Car Parking. Before selecting your beach for the day, a useful tip is to check the wind direction by looking at the weathercock on St. Mary's Church Spire in the centre of the town. If the wind is West, North West or South West, all the beaches will be fairly sheltered; if North or North Easterly the Castle Beach and South Beach are likely to be more sheltered; if East or South Easterly, then the Harbour Beach or North Beach will make that picnic a less sandy affair!

The Harbour

From early in the morning the tidal harbour is alive with activity and is a firm favourite for those who like to sit and watch. The old stone harbourside buildings and converted fisherman's cottages, together with the tiny St. Julian's Fishermen's Chapel and the Stone Quay with its mooring bollards, made from cannons, form a colourful backdrop to the bustle of the small craft within the harbour.

Many commercial boats ply to and from the Harbour carrying visitors to Caldey Island, on longer cruises around the bays and islands, or on fishing trips. The North bay is a superb sailing location and the active local sailing club, from its lovely old harbourside clubhouse built above the original fishmarket, hosts a number of regattas and Class sailing championships during the summer months, with Redwings, Lasers, GP14s and Miracles the main classes sailed. Visiting yachts can lie to anchor in the bay, or berth along the Quay wall, check with the harbourmaster's office above the harbour. Since the opening of new marinas at Neyland and Swansea, Tenby has become an even more popular weekend destination for yachtsmen.

The first stone quay was built in 1328 making it one of the earliest in Wales. To assist the town with the considerable expense incurred, Edward III granted permission for dues to be levied on all vessels using the port. The original pier was curved, and hooked round to the South towards the Mayor's Slip. It was built mainly to protect shipping from Northerly and Easterly gales and also for military reasons, most of the trade being carried on from the inner harbour wall, next to what is now the "sluice" (see p.13). For many years its most dominant feature was **St. Julian's Chapel**, built towards the outer end of the old quay.

During the Middle Ages, Tenby was second only to Bristol in its importance as a Bristol Channel port. Between 1550 and 1603 records indicate that Tenby's sea trade fell into

High tide Tenby Harbour. © *Alan Shepherd Transparency Library.*

two main categories:

1. Coastal Trade — with Bristol Channel ports such as Carmarthen, Milford, Minehead, Ilfracombe, and by far the most important — Bristol and Barnstaple. A little further afield trade was also conducted with Plymouth, Dartmouth and Ireland. The main commodities carried by these coastal craft often of about 10 tons displacement, were outwards — wool, woollen cloth, hides, lambswool and tanned leather, and on the return to Tenby — linen, calico, canvas, iron, pitch, soap, brass, pewter and haberdashery for the local housewives. To Ireland, coal, culm, corn and malt were exported, and horses, cattle, sawn timber, flax and iron imported.

2. Deep Water Trade — was conducted with France, Spain and Portugal. Salt, wine vinegar, oil for preserving and dried fruits such as raisins and prunes were imported. It is also exciting to note that in 1566 a ship from Aveiro (Portugal) brought salt, vinegar and "certain oranges with the mariners" — these are the earliest citrus fruit imports recorded in Wales. These blue water craft of up to 40 tons left the little port laden with cargoes of hides, wool, coarse woollen cloth and in later years, Welsh flannels. Later, the town's port trade declined dramatically and by the 19th Century it was little more than a fishing port. By this time the harbour

was dominated by Brixham and Dartmouth trawlers fishing for herring, and many West Country families settled in the area. All fishermen would assemble in the old St. Julian's Chapel before setting off for the fishing grounds. Prayers were offered for a good catch, and tithes of fish and oysters were paid to the clergyman in return for his services. Records inform us that this practice fell into disuse towards the end of the century when disputes arose between the fishermen and the incumbent!! The old St. Julian's Church became a bath house in 1781 and then a blacksmith's forge. It was destroyed in 1842.

The present stone quay was built in 1848 and the "new" picturesque St. Julian's Chapel was built, with the help of the fishing community in 1878 and is still generally referred to as "the Fishermen's Church". Some Sunday and weekday services are held and the church is open to the public during the summertime.

Small boats can be hired and there is a public slipway. An RNLI Inshore Lifeboat is on station. There is some car parking, but getting in

TENBY TELEPHONE NUMBERS

During the life of this Guide the telephone numbers of the Tenby Exchange will change. All existing 4-figure numbers will be prefixed by 84. The Area Code will remain 0834.

Fishing near the Lifeboat Station, Tenby. © A.S.T.L.

and out of the car park can be quite difficult in high season.

Castle Hill and the Prince Albert Memorial

This is the site of the original primitive settlement and later of the castle, first mentioned in 1153. Most of the walls and buildings have long been destroyed and today only the watch tower on the crest of the hill remains. This tower originally consisted of the circular tower only, the square tower which houses a spiral staircase was added later. From here a burning beacon would have been lit when danger threatened. Scraps of the Castle walls remain on the North side of the hill overlooking the lifeboat house, while the old gatehouse is still largely intact above the Rotary Garden on the approach path to the hill from the South. The buildings which now house the museum, and which were once a small school were originally part of the castle and may well have formed the living quarters, on the sunny South side of the fortress.

The Welsh National Memorial was unveiled in 1865 to commemorate the death of the Prince Consort, and was built largely through the enthusiasm of Joseph White, the then Mayor of Tenby, with the financial support of the Phillips family of Picton Castle.

Well worth a visit for the magnificent views afforded in all directions — to Worm's Head and the Gower Peninsula in the East and occasionally, on very clear days, beyond Caldey and St. Margaret's Islands to Lundy Island and the North coast of Devon. The cannons positioned around the summit of the hill are a few of the battery of 39 sited here, on the pier and in the "Gunfort Gardens" in 1797 to counter an invasion threat during the Revolutionary War. The private house also near the summit was previously used as the Coastguard House.

The Castle Hill also used to have a fashionable Iron Pier — The Royal Victoria Pier. This pier was completed and opened in 1897 for Queen Victoria's Jubilee. Two years

Prince Albert Memorial, Castle Hill. © A.S.T.L.

10

Aerial view of Tenby from the south. © *Alan Shepherd Transparency Library.*

later it had a second royal opening by the Duchess of York — later to become Queen Mary. The Duke was indisposed at Pembroke Dock. The pier was extensively used as an extension to the Castle Hill for promenading, also as an embarkation point for paddle steamer trips to Swansea and Ilfracombe and later for fishing competitions. The steps leading to the pier can still be located from the lower path to the East of the Lifeboat Slip. Sadly it was demolished in 1953. A replica of the Victorian bandstand which once stood on Castle Hill has recently been erected on the original site. It makes a delightful focal point for summer concerts, etc. Funds were raised entirely by voluntary activities amongst the local community.

The Lifeboat Station

Since its establishment in 1852 the Tenby Lifeboat has saved a great many lives. The old stone boathouse adjacent to the slipway to the Castle Beach has been replaced by the new house and slipway jutting into the North Bay from Castle Hill. Two loud rocket maroons herald the launch, a spectacular sight which never ceases to stir the imagination of young and old. The crew is made up from local boatmen, whose families have often had links with the Lifeboat service for

several generations. The Lifeboat House is open to the public most afternoons and evenings during the summer season.

In 1986 Tenby received a new Tyne Class Lifeboat. The new boat is named the Sir Galahad, in honour of the Welsh Guardsmen killed in the supply craft of the same name in the Falklands War.

Laston House

Situated immediately to the Eastern end of the stone quay. Commissioned in 1809 by Sir William Paxton, and rebuilt in 1810 after a fire, it had arrangements for hot and cold baths, and sea water baths were also available. The sea water baths were replenished by a reservoir of water, topped up at each high tide. The adjacent assembly rooms were a fashionable meeting place for the local "gentry" and the neighbouring cottages were built to house the bath attendants. The Greek inscription above the entrance door translates as "The sea washes away the ills of man".

* Laston House was probably so called because it marked the spot where the first quay was built and where the loading fee or Lastage was paid.

Tudor Merchant's House, Tenby.

St. Catherine's Fort

St. Catherine's Fort was completed in 1869 as part of a chain of forts built for the protection of the huge sheltered harbour at Milford Haven, the newly constructed Admiralty Ship Building Yards at Pembroke Dock and its naval anchorages. These forts were built on the orders of Lord Palmerston as part of a general contingency plan to counter the threat of invasion from any future enemy. Fortunately, these forts have never had to fire a shot in anger and are often referred to as "Palmerston Follies".

St. Catherine's Fort cost £50,000 to build and carried a complement of 100 men and their officers. When the foundations were excavated, an old chapel dedicated to St. Catherine, the patron saint of spinners, was discovered.

The Museum

A visit to Tenby Museum and Art Gallery is a "must", in its lovely setting in a restored part of the medieval buildings on Castle Hill.

There had already been 90 Mayors of Tenby before Columbus made his landfall in the New World in 1492. This wealth of history is brought into focus along with attractive displays devoted to early man, Tenby's relationship with the sea and the wildlife of Pembrokeshire.

But it is not like most museums. Run by volunteers, it is bright and cheerful and noted for its imaginative exhibitions. As you would expect in the birthplace of Augustus John, the art gallery is outstanding.

Don't miss it.

The Esplanade and St. Catherine's Fort from the South Beach.   © *Alan Shepherd Transparency Library.*

12

The Tudor Merchant's House

A well restored gabled house on olde-worlde Quay Hill. It has some fine Flemish chimneys and fireplaces. The ground floor houses the National Trust Information Centre. Just adjacent to the Tudor Merchant's House in Bridge Street is the former home of Charles Norris, the artist, many of whose fine paintings of old Tenby are housed in Tenby Museum. Several Norris paintings — on loan from the Tenby Museum collection — may also be viewed at the Tudor Merchant's House.

Open Easter-September, Mon.-Fri. 10.00-1.00, 2.30-6.00. Closed Sat.; Sun. 2.00-6.00pm.

The Sluice

This stone basin, just to the southern side of the harbour, was built in the 17th century as a dock for small boats. It also retained sea water brought into the harbour with the high tide and allowed this water to run slowly out again at low tide, thus scouring the area in front of the old wharf, ensuring that it did not not silt up with sand washed into the harbour during rough weather. Today it provides a useful safe winter mooring for some of the larger pleasure boats and private craft. The pool under the bridge is a good spot for children to fish for crabs at low water — providing mum or dad are at hand to supervise!

St. Mary's Church

Reputedly the largest parish church in Wales, with a fascinating history. The first church on this site was burnt down by the Welsh in 1186 only to be rebuilt and enlarged by Warren de Munchensey, Earl of Pembroke in 1245. A considerable amount of excellent recent restoration work has been undertaken on the church, the interior of which is surprisingly light and airy. It contains some interesting tombs which reflect the town's previous trading prosperity. The summer bustle of the town centre revolves around St. Mary's and with its spire standing at 152 feet high, it is a prominent feature on the skyline from all directions. In the evenings the exterior of the church is skilfully floodlit making a most attractive feature, with the illuminated spire rearing up into the night sky. Evening concerts given by local and visiting Male Voice Choirs and singers are held frequently in the church. A detailed guide by W. Gwyn-Thomas, M.A., is available inside the church.

The Town Walls

The Walls may have first been built by William de Valence, Earl of Pembroke, half brother of Henry III, who died in 1296. Originally the protective curtain of the town wall

St. Mary's Church, Tenby.

completely encircled the old town, extending from the Watch Tower on the cliffs above the South Beach to a similar tower above the North Bay. There was also probably a moat or ditch on the landward side, with a people's field beyond. In 1475 Jasper Tudor, Earl of Pembroke, assisted with the rebuilding and strengthening of the walls before presenting them to the town. Under Elizabeth I, subsidence of the wall foundations near the South Pool necessitated work to stablize and strengthen this section. This work was given

Five Arches, Tenby.

13

Belmont Arch — Town Walls, Tenby. © A.S.T.L.

Town Walls — St. Florence Parade.
   © Alan Shepherd Transparency Library.

Four Poster Bed in Tudor Merchant's House, Quay Hill.   © Alan Shepherd Transparency Library.

much greater significance by the growing threat posed by Spain. There is a small tablet, dated 1588, let into the wall opposite Tenby Garage to commemorate this. The intitials "H.H." stand for Howell Howell the then Mayor of Tenby.

The landward walls are still almost complete and lend the town a great deal of its character. Unfortunately most of the seaward defences extending from Castle Hill to the Southern end of the walls near the Imperial Hotel and from the Harbour to the old North Gate — where the Royal Lion Hotel now stands, have disappeared. Also gone are the two major fortified gates near the harbour — the Whitesands Gate, removed 1797 and the Quay Gate, removed in 1811.

The distinctive Five Arches was the original South West Gate. At first this entrance to the town consisted of a single simple archway through the main run of the wall, with no outer defences. Careful examination reveals the massive slats which housed the wooden bolts to the first gates. As defensive ideas became more sophisticated, the outer tower or barbican was constructed so as to force attackers to make a right-angled turn under heavy fire from above, before they could reach the inner wooden doorway. Look for the slot which carried the

portcullis in this original solitary outer arch (now the inner arch facing the War Memorial Gardens). The whole defensive structure was subsequently increased in height and the battlements and a parapet walk constructed. Finally, at the time of the French Revolutionary War, the walk was roofed over to provide all weather storage for arms and ammunition.

In 1873 the town corporation ordered the complete removal of the arches to speed traffic flow. However, this caused such an outcry that Dr. George Chater applied for an injunction from the Court of Chancery to prevent this work from being carried out. The council, now becoming aware of a growing groundswell of influencial opposition to the plan, thought better of their proposal and did not contest the injunction. The arches are now scheduled as an ancient monument and a tablet on the font of the gate tower records Dr. Chater's timely intervention.

The arch in St. Florence's Parade, near to the Imperial Hotel is the "Belmont Arch" and not an original feature. The seats along the length of the town walls in the South Parade provide a most welcome resting point after a busy day's sightseeing. Here the chestnut trees provide welcome shade from the hot sun.

THE TENBY DAFFODIL

The unique Tenby Daffodil was given its specific name Narcissus Obvallaris by R. A. Salisbury in 1796.

Between the years 1883-1885 it is reliably estimated that half a million bulbs from the fields around Tenby were dug up and exported to gardens in and around London. As a result this distinctive species was nearly exterminated.

Why was it so popular? Probably because of its hardy nature and dwarf stature, its especially brilliant uniform shade of yellow, and its ability to flower very early in the year. Even in hard winters it is usually in bloom by mid or late February.

Since the turn of the century, new horticultural techniques have produced endless new species of daffodil which allow the keen gardener to select those characteristics which appeal to him. This has allowed the Tenby daffodil, along with many other older varieties, to re-establish itself. Thankfully, it is now found in increasing numbers in older gardens, derelict cottage sites and village hedgerows, particularly in the Narberth, Meidrym and Crymmych areas.

North Beach and Goscar Rock.   © *Alan Shepherd Transparency Library.*

15

An Interesting Walk through the History of Tenby

Page references are given throughout to allow you to refer to the full information in the text. Each of the main features described in this walk is located by its reference number on the map.

St. Mary's Church, Tudor Square, St. Julian's Street, Castle Beach, Rotary Club Gardens, Tenby Castle and the Castle Hill, Tenby Museum, The Quay, Tenby Harbour and its Ancient Buildings, North Beach, The Croft, High Street.

● Start at St. Mary's Church (1), High Street. Use the High Street entrance to gain access to this beautiful church (p.13). Search out the plaque to **Robert Recorde**, a Tudor mathematician and scholar who was born in Tenby, and was one of the first academics to use the equals sign. Unfortunately, the picture on his medallion is probably **not** of Recorde.
● Emerge from the church by the same entrance and turn right down High Street and into Tudor Square, passing Woolworth's on your left.
● At the bottom right hand side of Tudor Square locate "Tenby House" (2). This was the home of **Sir William Paxton** from 1805-1824 (p.5).
● Continue down St. Julian's Street until you reach the "Hope and Anchor" pub on your left. Cross the road and find "East Rock House" (3). This was built by **Fulke Greville** who was primarily responsible for the layout and development of the port of Milford Haven. He was a nephew of Sir William Hamilton, husband of the famous Lady Emma Hamilton. In 1802 Sir William and Lady Hamilton, accompanied by Admiral Lord Nelson, came to Pembrokeshire probably at the invitation of Fulke Greville who

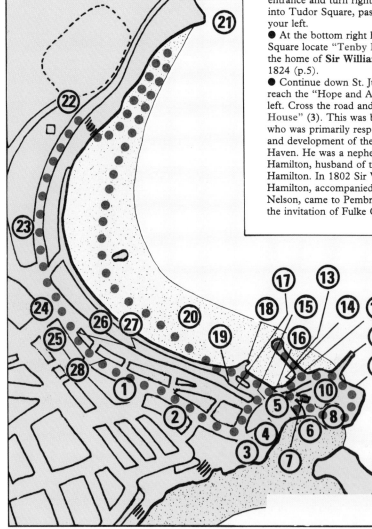

Castle Beach and St. Catherine's Fort. © A.S.T.L.

was anxious to enlist Nelson's support for his ambitious proposals to develop Milford Haven as a major commercial port and anchorage for the fleet. There is every likelihood that the party stayed at this house with its extensive clifftop views over the South Beach.

● Continue down St. Julian's Street, past the beautifully proportioned houses of **Lexden Terrace (4)** on your right — built in 1834 and arrive at St. Julian's Terrace (on your right) with its attractive Georgian houses in a variety of pastel colours overlooking the harbour. Note on No. 2 "Beach House" the old "Sun Fire Insurance" plaque — a timely reminder of the days before an organised fire service existed. A little further on, the last house on the right (No. 6), "Wide Horizons", merits closer attention. Originally called **"Hooper's Cot"** it was once the home of a Tudor sea captain and stood next to the **"Whitesand Gate" (5)**, which guarded the access from the harbour area to the town. The original house was removed with redevelopment around 1811 and the present building was used as a public baths — "the marine baths" — for a short period.

● Next bear to the right, under the arch and down the slipway towards the Castle Beach. **St. Catherine's Fort** is straight ahead. On your left

Fine Georgian Houses in St. Julian's St. Tenby. © A.S.T.L

Quay Hill, Tenby.   © *A.S.T.L.*

Castle Gateway — Castle Hill, Tenby. © *A.S.T.L.*

● Continue past the white painted "Laston House" (12) with its Greek inscription (p.11) and neighbouring cottages. The short stretch of road which brings you back to **Castle Square** was built shortly after 1811 to allow the carriages of the "gentry" to reach the fashionable **Assembly Rooms**. Proceed past the **First Aid Post**, and the **Harbour Master's Office**. The office is on the site of the original weighbridge, once much in use, when the harbour had a busy commercial life. Turn sharp right and onto the **old stone quay**. Further on are the stone steps from which the commercial boats shuttle visitors to and from Caldey Island, and the larger boats embark passengers for cruises. Always plenty of activity here when the tide is in.

● If the tide is out, descend the steps and make your way through the assortment of craft and moorings to the "Seamen's Chapel" (14) (p.9-10), at the top of the Harbour Beach.

● If the tide is in, retrace your steps to Castle Square, turn right at the Harbour Master's Office, and the chapel is now below you on your right.

● Standing outside the entrance to **St. Julian's Chapel,** look up to your right. The arches which now support a picturesque garden with some lovely fuchsia hedges were built by Sir William Paxton around 1813. Originally they supported "Paxton"s Road" (15) which was designed to provide a better link between the harbour and Crackwell Street, but plans were changed and a new high level road above Paxton's was built. The supporting arches are now used as garages and stores by boatmen and residents of the harbour area.

● Walk on past the site of the old "Harbour Gate" (16), demolished in 1811, and through the crowded little car park, where the quaint old stores on your left were once **fishermen's cottages.** Leave **Tenby Sailing Club** on your left and continue across the lifting bridge over the entrance to the "sluice" (p.13). On the other side of the sluice surrounded by parked sailing dinghies, the reconstructed building is the Tenby

near the bottom of the slip, the grey stone building is the original lifeboat house (6), in use between 1895 and 1905.

● Return up the slip and turn right, past the entrance to the **Rotary Club Garden**, and pass through the old Castle Gateway (7) ahead. Note the slots for the portcullis in the second archway on your left.

● Carry straight on and pass the Tenby Museum and Art Gallery (8) on your left.

● Climb the few steps and you are now on **Castle Hill** with its new replica of the original Victorian Bandstand. On your right you have a fine view of St. Catherine's Island and the Fort — and can now appreciate the full majestic 1.5 mile sweep of the South Sands as they fall away to **Giltar Point** in the distance.

● Bear right and follow the lower pathway around the perimeter of the hill for another 100 yards or so until a flight of stone steps appears rather mysteriously on your right — leading apparently to the rocks below. This was the entrance to the Royal Victoria Pier (9), (p.10).

● Take the next fork on the left which climbs up to the summit of the hill. **The ancient watch tower,** the old Coastguard House, cannon and the Prince Albert Memorial (10) now claim your attention.

● Retrace your steps to the lower path, turn left and visit the Lifeboat House (11) if possible.

Pet Shop

TENBY MARKET
HIGH STREET
TENBY

☆ *Pet Foods*
☆ *Leather Goods*
☆ *Walking Sticks*
☆ *Pet Accessories*

Sea Cadets' Base. It used to be called "Sleeman's Stores" (17) after a wine importer from Bristol who used it as his warehouse.

● As you walk on along the outer sluice wall, look upwards and to your left and you will notice a steep flight of stone steps descending through the trees. These are known locally as **"Dead Man's Steps"** because until fairly recently the town mortuary was sited in the top arch to the right of the steps.

● On your right, the wide concrete launching slipway is called the Mayor's Slip (18), so named after a former Mayor — Clement Williams who built the original much smaller ramp at his own expense. This in turn replaced

an earlier much cruder barrier of huge boulders which was built out towards the old pier to protect the craft in the harbour from what is known locally as "a Run". This is in effect a great inward surge of water into the harbour which accompanies large waves driven into the North Bay by winds from the East and the North East. This barrier of large rocks also had a military role. From its seaward extremity a chain could be stretched right across the harbour to the pier. This barrier was known as the **Barricados**.

● Immediately behind the Mayor's Slip is the Tenby RNLI Inshore Lifeboat Boathouse (19). An inflatable inshore craft has been on station since 1971 and has saved many lives off the local beaches and cliffs, in situations where the much greater sea going capacity of the **"Sir Galahad"** is not required. Usually manned by a crew of two or three, the current D class craft, "Charlie B" was given to the town in 1986 by the Misses Moira and Sheila Barrie, in memory of their father, Charles Barrie. Over £20,000 was raised to pay for the Boathouse by residents of Tenby and Saundersfoot areas. Above the Boathouse is a very pleasant sitting-out area — particularly sunny in the mornings.

● If the tide is out, either continue your stroll along the **North Walk** or descend the steps to the beach and continue along the **North Sands**.

Medieval Sun Alley — between High St. and Crackwell St.   © A.S.T.L.

The Gardens on Paxton's Road.
© Alan Shepherd Transparency Library.

19

Notice that on this side of the town the cliffs are composed of much softer rocks, mainly shales, than the South side. As a result they are more unstable, require more maintenance and **must not be used for climbing.**

● The metal post which marks the only rocky obstruction near the entrance to the harbour is known locally as "the Barrel Post" (20).

● On reaching the "Barrel Post" look to your left and locate the area of cliff below the Royal Gatehouse Hotel. A large section of this cliff subsided some years ago, tragically killing two people who were on the North Walk at the time. Extensive construction work has now been carried out on the cliffs surrounding the North Beach to stabilise these dangerous cliff faces and ensure safety for the public.

● On reaching **Gosgar Rock** either bear left and climb the zig zag slipway to the Norton, or continue along the North Beach towards the First Point (21). This is the rust coloured rocky bluff at the end of the beach with the attractive red and white house "Nyth Aderyn" (birds nest) spectacularly placed above. On the final section of the beach note the new sections of sea defences built recently, with their enormous granite boulders.

● Return partially along the beach, then via the new steps to North Cliff (22) where you can regain your breath after the climb by admiring

North Beach and First Point, Tenby. © *Alan Shepherd Transparency Library.*

20

South Beach from St. Catherine's Fort.

one of the finest views Tenby has to offer.
● Make your way back to St. Mary's along the
Croft and past the Information Centre (23).
More municipal gardens with magnificent views
on your left. Continue up the Norton until you
reach the Royal Lion Hotel on your right. Here
stood the Great North Gate (24) of the old
walled town, which was finally pulled down in
1782 following an order of the council in 1781.
In the basement of the Hotel are some remains of
the gate and the town walls, together with an old
well.
● Stay on the outside pavement near the edge of
the cliff and note the premises opposite which
now houses "County Clothes" (25). This
interesting building received an "Award of
Commendation" for its design in the 1851
Exhibition at the Crystal Palace, London.
● For photographers, the gardens which hug the
edge of the cliff, opposite Stephen Davies'
provide one of the best vantage points for
panoramic views of the harbour and Castle Hill.
These gardens also follow the line of the old
Northern Walls which at one time ran from the
Great North Gate to the Harbour Gate. The
"Candy" Restaurant just ahead of you is thought
to be built on one of the small towers (26)
which punctuated the Northern seaward defences
of the town.
● Pause for a moment to cast a coin into the
Rotary Club "Wishing Well" in the Gardens,
and of course make an appropriate wish!
● At the junction of Crackwell Street and High
Street note the clock in the wall above the

LITTLE ENGLAND BEYOND WALES

*An extract from George Owen's
"Elizabethan Pembrokeshire," written at the end
of the 16th century.*

*"The said county of Pembrokeshire is
usually called Little England Beyond Wales, and
that not unworthily, and therefore I think good to
show my opinion why the same was so called. Mr.
Camden calleth it Anglia Transwallia. The
reasons why it took that name may be well
conjectured for that the most part of the country
speaketh English, and in it no use of the Welsh.
The names of the people are mere English, each
family following the English fashion in surnames.
The buldings are English like in townreds and
villages and not in several and lone houses. Their
diet is as the English people use, as the common
food beef, mutton , pig, lamb, veal and kid, which
usually the poorest husbandman doth daily feed
on. The names of the county places are altogether
English as Wiston, Picton, Haroldson, Robeston . .
. so that a stranger travelling from England and
having ridden four score miles and more in Wales,
having heard no English nor English names of
people or of places and coming hither to
Pembrokeshire where he shall hear nothing but
English . . . would think that Wales were
environed with England, and would imagine that
he had travelled through Wales and come into
England again. These reasons and also that most
of the ancient gentlemen came thither out of
England . . . might very fittingly procure it the
name of "Little England Beyond Wales."*

South Beach looking towards Giltar Point.
© Alan Shepherd Transparency Library.

Morning Sunshine on The Croft.   *© A.S.T.L.*

Enjoying the view from the High Street Gardens.

Greengrocer's shop. Once known as Clock House (27), until recently the "Corporation" was responsible for the clock, and employed a local watch maker to wind it up and keep it in good repair.

● Return to St. Mary's via **High Street**. The wide pavement on your right as you approach St. Mary's was the site of some rather nice town houses belonging to wealthy merchants until the 19th century, when they were demolished to help reduce traffic congestion. Subsequently this area was used as a **small market** for fruit and vegetables. This section of the High Street, together with Tudor Square, is supported on many **very ancient cellars**, used at one time for storing goods. One local rumour has it that it was through one of these cellars that Henry Tudor was spirited away to the Harbour, and then to Brittany on a ship owned by Thomas White the then mayor. Note "Boots" the Chemist shop opposite the church — part of a property called Jasperley House (28), after the medieval **Mayor Jasperly White**.

1. Medical Assistance
Doctors: The Health Centre, Narberth Road, Tenby. Tel: 4161/2.
Dentists: J.G. French and K.R. Bevan, 5 The Norton, Tenby. Tel: 2035.
Clifton Rock Dental Practice, Greenhill Road, Tenby. Tel: 3600.
Optician: J. Stevenson, 2 Deer Park, Tenby. Tel: 2384.
Chiropodist: Merrie Feet, Newton House, Harding Street, Tenby. Tel: 3217.
Hospital: Trafalgar Rd., Tenby. Tel: 2040.
Community Clinic: Warren Street, Tenby. Tel: 2991.

2. Animal Welfare
Veterinary Surgery: Marsh Farm, Marsh Road, Tenby. Tel: 2278.

3. Information Agencies
Tourist Information Centre: The Croft, Tenby. Tel: 2402/3510.
Pembrokeshire Coast National Park Centre, Kilgetty. Tel: 813672 & 812175 (Comprehensive summer programme of walks and talks).
South Pembrokeshire Information Centre, Kilgetty. Tel: 813672.
Local Papers (1) Tenby Observer, every Friday; provides comprehensive coverage of all local news, events, etc. plus tide table.
(2) **Western Telegraph,** every Wednesday.

4 Evening Entertainment
De Valence Pavilion, Upper Frog Street, Tenby. (Summer shows, discos, roller discos, choral concerts, etc).
St. Mary's Church. Excellent summer programme of choral concerts, organ recitals, etc.
The Torch Theatre, Milford Haven. (See local press for details).
Warren Bingo Club, Warren Street, Tenby. Throughout the summer season, many of the local organisations produce a wide variety of events in and around Tenby in aid of charity, e.g. lifeboat/helicopter air sea rescue demonstrations, aerobatic displays, fêtes, dog shows, etc. Details in local press.

5. Clubs
Rotary Club — Royal Gate House Hotel, Tenby. Tel: 2255.

Round Table — Royal Gate House Hotel, Tenby. Tel: 2255.
Lions International Club — Giltar Hotel, The Esplanade, Tenby. Tel: 3293.
British Legion — Lower Frog Street, Tenby. Tel: 2307.
Ex-Servicemen's Club — South Parade, Tenby. Tel: 2258.
Tenby United R.F.C. — Upper Frog Street, Tenby. Tel: 3501.

6. Local Bus/Coach Services
(Day Trips and Tours)
Silcox — The Arcade, Upper Frog Street, Tenby (bookings also for National Express)
Tenby Coaches — Nelson's Walk, Upper Frog Street, Tenby.
British Rail — Tenby Railway Station, Warren Street, Tenby. Tel: 2248.

7. General Information
Library — Greenhill Avenue, Tenby. Tel: 3934.
Police Station — Warren Street, Tenby. Tel: 2302.
Post Office — Warren Street, Tenby. (Last collection for most major towns 6.00 p.m.; Sat. 1.45 p.m.; Sunday 1.00 p.m.

8. Sports Facilities
Tenby Bowling Club — 1 South Cliff Street, Tenby (also Putting Green for family).
Sea Fishing/Boat Cruises — Book at harbourside kiosks.
Golf — 18-hole championship links course. Tenby Golf Club. Tel: 2787.
Horse Riding/Pony Trekking — Details from Information Centres.
Sailing Club — The Harbour, Tenby. Tel: 2762.
Swimming Pool — Marsh Road, Tenby. Tel: 3575 for opening times.
Diving — Dragon Divers, Castle Beach, Tenby.
Tennis Courts — Available at Greenhill School, Heywood Lane, Tenby, during the school holidays.

Tenby Telephone Numbers
During the life of this Guide the telephone numbers of the Tenby exchange will change. All exisiting 4-figure numbers will be prefixed by 84. The area code will remain 0834.

SHOPPING IN TENBY

Shopping in Tenby

Tudor Square, Tenby. © *Alan Shepherd Transparency Library.*

Caldey and St. Margaret's Islands

Caldey Island from the air.   © *Alan Shepherd Transparency Library.*

Since the first visitors began to arrive in South Pembrokeshire, by overland coach, these glorious islands have tempted travellers of all ages with their spectacular beauty and rich wildlife. Lying just far enough away to provoke a well founded sense of promise and adventure, they beckon tantalisingly, and reward the curious visitor with a very special brand of island magic.

A Day out on Caldey

The island, which lies some three miles from Tenby Harbour, forms a highly effective natural breakwater for the beaches of Tenby. It is one and a half miles long, and little under threequarters of a mile wide.

History

Monks of one sort or another have lived and worked on Caldey for 1,500 years. The original Welsh name of **Ynys Pyr** — the Island of Pyro - preserves the name of the first Abbot from the 6th century. During the 10th century the settlements of the Pembrokeshire coast were terrorised by the Norsemen, and the name

Caldey, or "Cold Island" derives from this period.

The early history of the island dates back to 8,000 b.c. with human remains, early flint tools, and the bones of animals long since extinct in Britain, being excavated by one of the monks. In 1113, Henry I of England made a gift of the island to Robert Fitzmartin, a Norman nobleman who promptly gave it to his mother, Geva. In 1136 it was given to the Benedictine monks of the Abbey of Tiron in France, who had already founded an abbey at St. Dogmaels, near Cardigan. Their **new priory** was built on the site of Pyro's earlier primitive monastic settlement. It was a building of great strength, and is still largely intact today. Nearby, the island spring was channelled into a series of ponds, and a little further down stream the water was used for turning a small corn mill. At the same time, the round stone **Watch Tower** above Priory Bay was built. From here the Priory, with its own considerable defences, could be forewarned of approaching danger.

In 1536 Henry VIII dissolved the Monasteries, and the Benedictines on Caldey were expelled. **John Bradshaw of Presteigne** became the new owner. In 1597 ownership passed to **Walter Philpin, Mayor of Tenby in**

1601, and he in turn sold it to **Reeve Williams and Robert Williams in 1653. The Earl of Warwick** next bought the island for £3000 in 1786, and twelve years later it was sold to one of its most illustrious owners, **Thomas Kynaston of Pembroke**, Kynaston built a handsome mansion in the grounds of the Priory, and probably added many of the farm buildings which are in existence today. From the outset it was Kynaston's intention to exploit the fine Caldey limestone to take advantage of the current boom in building and road making. There were already four old quarries in existence, but the Kynaston family developed the huge quarry at High Cliff from which eventually 20,000 tons of limestone per year were exported. **James Hawkesley** purchased the island for £15,950 in 1867. Hawkesley was young, intelligent, and enthusiastically embraced the new, more scientific approach to agriculture, which was then emerging. By all accounts he was a fair and extremely popular employer. Under his guidance the emphasis of the island farm changed from stock breeding to market gardening. Vast greenhouses, heated by steam, were built and to transport the produce to market, Hawkesley bought a 75 ton ketch which traded with Swansea and Pembroke, as well as Tenby. A High Sheriff of Pembrokeshire and an Alderman of Tenby, he died in 1891 at the early age of 52. It is reported that when news of his

Father Dèsirè at work in the Perfumery. © *ASTL.*

death reached the men working in the limestone quarries they immediately lay their tools down and made their way home, as a mark of respect.

In 1894 the island passed briefly into the hands of Thomas Smith Cunninghame who bought it for £12,750 before disposing of it for £12,200 in 1897. The new owner was the **Reverend Done Bushell**, senior maths teacher, housemaster and subsequently Chaplain at Harrow, the famous public school. Bushell, who had ten children, bought Caldey as a holiday home and for the benefit of his mentally handicapped son who he felt needed to be protected from an unfriendly world. During the relatively short period of his ownership this scholarly man undertook a costly programme of

The Abbey, Caldey Island.   © *Alan Shepherd Transparency Library.*

29

renovation on the Old Priory, St. Illtud's and St. David's Churches.

In 1906 the island was sold to an **Anglican Benedictine Brotherhood, under Dom Aelred Carlyle,** once again at a heavy loss to the previous owner. Carlyle, who appears to have been a rather awkward character, lacking business acumen, immediately set about a vast building programme. Further restoration was carried out at the Priory Church, a Guest House (now St. Philomena's), was built, together with a row of small workmen's cottages on top of the low cliff above the village. A shop, club room, village hall, and the houses known as Ty Gwyn and Ty Mair were also constructed. The present day monastery was built between 1910 and 1913 using stone brought by tramway from High Cliff Quarry. Here Carlyle had invested in expensive equipment, and in a new jetty for loading ships. In 1913, Dom Aelred and 22 of his monks were received into the Catholic Church, and in 1914 he was appointed Abbot. At about the same time, on the outbreak of World War I, the first detachment of Coastguards arrived on the island. Dom Aelred resigned his office in 1921 (with the community £20,000 in debt), and seven years later the Benedictines moved to Prinknash, near Gloucester. **In 1924 the island was sold for the last time to the present order of Reformed Cistercians, and in January 1929 the advance party of monks from the Abbey of Chimay in Belgium settled in residence.**

Visitors embarking for Caldey Island from the Castle Beach, Tenby. © A.S.T.L.

Approaching the Landing Jetty on Caldey. © ASTL

Exploring the Island

Landing on Caldey is now a simple affair. In 1958 the jetty was extended by sinking old wartime barges made of concrete to extend the slipway on Priory Bay seawards. In peak season passengers arriving at the island at extreme low water may be off-loaded on to an ex-army amphibious landing craft to cover the last 30 yards to the jetty, much to the excitement of the children aboard.

Which parts of Caldey are open to visitors?

Visitors to the island are asked to limit themselves to the clearly marked paths. In particular they are asked to respect the privacy of the monastery enclosure. The dangerous nature of the cliffs, blowholes and deep fissures, together with a need to protect the resident population of sea birds and their clifftop habitat, are the important reasons behind the Abbot's request.

Priory Bay

As you walk towards the village and pass

Low Water Landing on Caldey using the 'Dukw'

The Community at Prayer in the Monastery Church   © *Alan Shepherd Transparency Library*

the cliff on your right, remember that until around 1850, the area now covered by the dunes and much of the low land immediately behind (The Common), was a shallow arm of the sea. Note the marker post for the mains power cable, laid to the Island in 1965.

The Village

As you emerge from the shady wooded area which borders the Northern edge of the village, note the right turn which doubles back up a slope. This narrow lane, with its fuchsia hedges, passes the **lime kiln** (once a windmill), and rises to the elevated ground above the Western end of Priory Bay. On the right lies (1) **St. Philomena's**, The Island Guest House, and a little further on (2) **the Calvary**, with its distant views of Caldey Sound framed by banks of yellow gorse and (3) **The Chapel of our Lady of Peace - formerly the watch tower**.

Within the village you will find the **Monastery Tea Rooms**, the village pond, the tasteful **Island Gift Shop** where many of the items on sale are made by the monks or by their colleagues from other monastic communities. Just a few yards on is the statue of **"Our Lady of Walsingham"**. This delightful shrine was given to the island by a former resident, Mrs. Stanton, and is always kept decorated with wild flowers by the ladies of the village. It lies in what was the **old village pump house**.

The Perfume Shop. Here is the most intriguing

of the various business ventures undertaken by the monastery. The range of sophisticated perfume and toiletries is partially made from the profusion of wild flowers and gorse which gives Caldey its special, almost Mediterranean, air. The subtle fragrances which fill the air and waft over you as you enter the perfumery ensure that at least one member of the family will linger . . . and linger!

Opposite the Perfume Shop the **Island Post Office** will frank your holiday postcards with the unique **Caldey imprint**.

Post Office, Caldey.   © *A.S.T.L.*

31

Monk's Timetable

3.15 a.m.	Rise
3.30 a.m.	VIGILS
6.30 a.m.	LAUDS & CONCELEBRATED MASS
	Breakfast
8.50 a.m.	TERCE
	Work or Study
12.15 p.m.	SEXT
	Dinner
1.50 p.m.	NONE
	Work or Study
5.30 p.m.	VESPERS
	Supper
7.30 p.m.	COMPLINE
	Retire

Bear round to the left, follow the narrow roadway which skirts the bottom of the old quarry, past the colourful rose beds and the row of neat cottages, some of which were **once used**

A Visitor's Guide to Caldey Island

All visitors considering taking a day trip to Caldey and / or cruise around Caldey and St. Margaret's Islands should obtain a copy of this publication by the present author. It is the only comprehensive guide available to the two islands and it will help you and your family to make the most of a very special day out.

by the coastguards who resided on the island. After passing the buildings used for manufacturing the Caldey Perfumes, you will now reach the statue of **St. Samson, the patron saint of the island** — the Abbey and its Church are dedicated to him. He was the second Abbot of the original community, after the ill-fated Pyro, who, records reveal, died after a bout of drunkeness, culminating with him wandering around the monastery grounds before falling into the pond!!! St. Samson was a thoroughly Godly man and eventually left Caldey to work in Ireland before setting up a monastery at Dol in Brittany where he became the first Bishop. In 1919 a small part of St. Samson's relics were returned to Caldey.

Castle Beach and St. Catherine's Fort.

St. David's Church. © A.S.T.L.

St. Illtud's Church. © A.S.T.L.

St. David's Church

This is just a few yards further on your left. It is the parish church of the island. During the early years of the island there is plenty of evidence to indicate that it was used as a refuge against the Vikings - and also later against raids by the pirates who infested the Severn Sea. Some restoration work took place in 1836 and the building was used as a blacksmith's forge for a time. In 1906 Done Bushell restored the interior to its present state and the attractive red tiled roof was added later.

Beyond it lie the Monastery Gardens and workshops which are not open to the public. The assembly point for the guided tours of the monastery (men only), is straight ahead at the main door of the Monastery.

St. Illtud's Church and The Old Priory

Retrace your steps to the island Post Office, turn left and set off under hedges laced with the red and purple of wild fuchsia, towards St. Illtud's Church, the Old Priory and the farm. The Old Priory and St. Illtud's Church encapsulate within their walls the entire Christian history of the island.

After the dissolution of the monasteries, the buildings were used as a malt house, forge, barn and laundry, until being restored by Done Bushell (note the brass plaque in the porch). The choir stalls and other furnishings were made by the Anglican Benedictines early this century. **Locate the Ogham stone** which stands close to the stained glass window at the South side of the nave. There is some dispute as to the exact translation of the inscription, but the stone would appear to date from the 6th century, when St. Samson was Abbot. As you leave this quaint little church note (a) the uneven floor of pebbles and beach stones; (b) the gatehouse and dovecote of the Old Priory on the left of the yard; (c) the

The Village Green, the Gift Shop and the Island Perfume Shop. © A.S.T.L.

Island Cottages adjacent to the Village Green. © A.S.T.L.

heavy fortified spire, which leans over 40 inches from the perpendicular.

The Monastery Farm

Most of the overall 550 acres of the island is farmed by the monks and their helpers. The dairy herd of 22 Jersey cows is the most important part of the farm economy, with the high quality milk converted into yoghurt, butter, chocolate, ice cream, cream, cheese cakes, etc. A small beef suckler herd is also maintained to provide income, and the island's arable land is

Sandtop Beach.

used mainly for oats and barley, grown as feed. A few pigs and sheep are kept, but the sheep have proved very difficult to keep under control, and many have been lost over the cliffs. The straw from the arable corps is utilised as fuel for the "straw burning" boiler which heats the monastery.

The Lighthouse

This dominates the whole of the Southern side of the island from its magnificent vantage point 188 feet above sea level at Chapel Point. The lighthouse and its compound, owned by Trinity House, is now fully automatic. The light

The Lighthouse at Chapel Point.

is gas burning and is programmed to respond to the natural increase and decrease of daylight. It was built in 1828.

The well drained grassy slopes, with their drifts of dwarf yellow gorse, in front of the lighthouse, form one of the best picnic sites on the entire island. The views from here are stunning. To the East Worm's Head, at the seaward end of the Gower Peninsula, lies some 19 miles away. To the South, on a clear day, the steep cliffs and flat topped profile of Lundy Island appear as a blue-grey form 27 miles away on the horizon. To the West, the line of cliffs, bays and headlands terminate at the blunt slab of St. Govan's head.

Bathing on Caldey

Priory Beach is the only safe bathing beach on Caldey. The beach is excellent with a range of dunes of fine powdery sand just inland. There are no facilities of any kind, but the village with toilets, refreshments, etc., is just a few hundred yards away. When swimming, please keep well away from the landing stage which is usually quite busy with arrivals and departures. It is also recommended that you only swim parallel to the beach, as more than a hundred yards offshore the spring tides can run strongly. This beach was used by the island's coal boats which were beached at the top of the tide and then unloaded their important cargo bucket by bucket into

CALDEY ABBEY
CALDEY ISLAND, OFF TENBY

When you visit this beautiful Monastery Island, just 20 minutes by boat from Tenby Harbour, do come and see the delightful range of Island Products – *

PERFUMES and COLOGNES – The Monks of Caldey Island have been making perfumes for the past 20 years and their skills are respected nationally and internationally.

DAIRY PRODUCTS – Yoghurts, cream, butter, cheeses etc. made on the Island from the Monastery's Jersey herd.

CHOCOLATE – Handmade Milk and Plain Chocolate, made by the Monks from the finest ingredients.

Also available from the Caldey Abbey Shop in Tudor Square, Tenby.

Price lists and information on Postal Services from:–The Perfumery, Caldey Island, off Tenby, Pembrokeshire (please enclose S.A.E.)

CALDEY IS OPEN TO THE PUBLIC MAY-SEPTEMBER. REGULAR BOAT SERVICE FROM TENBY HARBOUR.

Caldey and St. Margaret's Additional Information

Getting there: *A fleet of boats runs to the Island from Tenby Harbour, from about the Spring Bank Holiday to late September. These boats, which are strictly supervised by the Ministry of Transport, are owned by local boatmen, many of whom are members of the crew of Tenby Lifeboat. Tickets for Caldey are obtained from the Booking Kiosk in Castle Square above the harbour. Having purchased a ticket you can travel and return on any boat, as they are all part of the same "pool." The crossing takes approximately 30 minutes, and boats run every 15 minutes between 9.30 a.m. and 4.00 p.m. Mon. - Fri. At high tide all boats leave from Harbour, and at low tide from the temporary landing stage on the Castle Beach.*

Caldey Island Shop: *Quay Hill, Tenby. All island products on sale, as well as on the island.*

Dogs: *These are allowed but must be kept on a lead at all times.*

---

horse drawn carts. A walk round the first point at the Eastern end of the beach reveals the raised beach, the massive High Cliff quarry and the remains of the old loading facilities.

Landing on Caldey - Private Pleasure Craft

Landing on any part of Caldey from craft other than those in the 'Caldey Pool' is only permitted with the permission of the Abbot. Boat owners are (a) reminded that the Island is closed to all visitors on Sundays; (b) asked to respect the privacy of those beaches which lie within the monastery enclosure, e.g. Bullum's Bay.

ACKNOWLEDGEMENTS

The author would like to acknowledge that much of the material for this part of the Guide has been gleaned from the original research by the well known local author Roscoe Howells. Roscoe's two fascinating books on the Island. "Total Community" and "Caldey" form the most authoritative literary sources available on all aspects of island history and life.

I would also like to thank Brother Robert, Abbot of Caldey, for his help in providing additional useful information incorporated in this section.

Father Robert processing accounts on his computer.
© Alan Shepherd Transparency Library.

Saundersfoot

The Village Beach, looking East over the Harbour.

Bonvilles Court Colliery

Saundersfoot Harbour, 1908.

History

Saundersfoot lies some three miles North of Tenby and is a much newer settlement, tucked beside the impressive curve of Saundersfoot Bay. In 1600 Sannders Foot was a small manor in the great forest of Coedrath which covered much of this part of Pembrokeshire. By the end of the 18th Century it was a sleepy little fishing village shipping out the occasional cargo of coal. By 1810 the coal trade had grown considerably and it became a thriving coal exporting port.

The harbour was built between 1829 and 1834 at a cost of £7,000. Rail links to six local collieries brought the high grade anthracite coal to the harbour for loading on to small coasters. By 1845 up to 20,000 tons were exported annually from one colliery alone. A little later, using locally discovered iron ore from the rust brown cliffs between Saundersfoot and Amroth, an ironworks was established at Stepaside. Part of the Stepaside Ironworks can still be seen within the pleasant confines of the Heathfield Court Caravan Park. The tunnels in the

36

Miner's Train passes through Railway Street.

cliff path to the East of Saundersfoot were built to carry the railway servicing the trade. The street now called "The Strand", was called "Railway Street" and the Barbecue Restaurant was originally the colliery offices. In "A Guide to Tenby and its Neighbourhood", by R. Mason in 1863, he describes a visit to Saundersfoot as follows: "We are now in the land of coal and culm, we see two collieries at work, the fair sex with wheelbarrows conveying the material from the pit mouth to its temporary destination, while men and boys fill cradle after cradle below to be drawn to the light by the steam engine which presides over the works". (Refers to the Bonville's Court Mine which closed in 1930 and

Loading Coal, Saundersfoot Harbour.

All black and white pictures in this Saundersfoot section are taken from "Old Saundersfoot", by courtesy of the author Roscoe Howells. This excellent book contains a wealth of historical information and rare illustrations on the history of Saundersfoot and the surrounding villages. Available from local bookshops.

Loading Coal, Saundersfoot Harbour, 1937.

Harbour at sunrise.   *Photography: Mr. V. Walters.*

is now a modern caravan park.) However, the thin and erratic nature of the deposits of both minerals left the area unable to compete with the ever growing South Wales fields and by 1900 mining had declined. In 1939 the final two major pits closed and tourism, which had been growing since the turn of the century, now became the lifeblood of the village.

Today there is very little evidence of this industrial heritage and the village lies in a lovely sheltered valley, overlooked from the North by the landscaped and well wooded grounds of Hean Castle which from 1863-1899 was the home of the main local mine owners - the Vickerman family. In summer the village is a bustling little place full of shops, restaurants, cafès, pubs and and with a wide variety of accommodation.

* Those with a special interest in the history of this interesting area can buy "A Walk Through The Pembrokeshire Coalfield", National Park publication.

The **Harbour** is large and sheltered from the open sea by two large stone breakwaters. It nestles, secure from the South Westerly gales behind a high cliff to the South and the entrance channel is kept clear for the harbour traffic by the periodic flushing of a large sluice of fresh

Railway Street, 1900 (now The Strand).

Local Miners digging coal on the beach during the strike of 1922.

The Rosalind.

Between 1840 and 1842, R. H. Franks visited many of the mines in the Saundersfoot district, on behalf of the Commission of Enquiry, (Employment of Children). The following information is largely extracted from his report.

At Broadmoor Colliery the proprietor, Lewis Wilson, reported that there was no fixed age for the children to begin working in his mine. Boys began around seven years old, though children of six were occasionally employed. James Bowen, a Narberth surgeon, had already noted that the average life expectancy of a collier was 40 years, rarely 45, and he was highly critical of the use of child labour, believing that it shortened their lives. Wilson disagreed, claiming that, "A limitation of age would be a barrier to their being brought up to working habits."

Children were used mostly for '"tramming" — pulling and pushing coal trams. Because many of the coal seams in the Saundersfoot mines were narrow and badly faulted, the "mainways" — passages to the coal face — were often of such small dimensions that only children could work in them. Leaving these passages small also saved a great deal of extra cutting and propping, and thus reduced the colliery managers' additional expenses. In 1842, at Broadmoor, a tram carried 4.5 cwt. of coal, at neighbouring Begelly, 5.5 cwt. These were usually moved by not more than two children. In those parts of the shafts which were too restricted even for tramming, children would revert to the earlier methods of hauling sledges, skips or tubs. These contained around 1.5 cwt. of coal. One child pushed, while the other pulled. The "puller" wore the hated rope girdle attached to which was a length of chain. This passed between his legs and was fastened to a metal eye on the skip. He then crawled on hands and knees while his partner pushed from behind. In the Hean Castle Colliery, the girdle and chain was replaced by a heavy wooden handle called a "Goff."

There were no agreements as to how many hours the children could work, and the colliery owners claimed that 9-10 hours a day was the average.

Franks report disputes this and found the average to be 12 hours, with cases recorded where some children had worked for 14, 15 and even 16 hours a day. In this incredibly long working shift there were no provisions of any sort for regular meal breaks. Children ate their meagre bread and cheese wherever and whenever they could. Lewis Wilson of Broadmoor admitted that when the collliery was especially busy children were required to work on the night shift. Richard Buckby, the Rector of Begelly, stated that children often left school at the age of 10 and that there was no educational provision for children employed in labour. He added, "If such schools did exist it would be difficult to persuade colliers to send their children to them."

The following simple statements by two young children, recorded by Franks, portray vividly the brutality of their daily existence underground. James Davies, aged 8, worked in the Hean Castle Pit, owned by Thomas Stokes. "I have been below one year and I earn 10d. a week which my father takes. I work with my brother who is eleven, pushing trams. I have never been hurt, and I work longer than my father. I have been to Sunday School but never to day school." Benjamin Thomas, another 8 year old, was employed at Broadmoor Colliery. He described the work as very hard and added, "My father is dead and my mother works in the colliery with my sister and three brothers. None of the boys in this pit wear shoes." Bear in mind also that most of the colliers in South Pembrokeshire went home to country cottages, with large gardens or a few acres of ground and a cow and a pig. Meagre wages were, thus, eked out with home grown produce. After finishing their backbreaking shifts down the mine and often walking several miles home, children were then expected to shoulder their share of the work around the "smallholding." Little wonder that by the time they reached their teens many of these tough little characters looked weary and care-worn.

THE SAUNDERSFOOT BRITISH SCHOOL

After raising money and collecting donations for several years, the school was opened for instruction on Monday, 10th January, 1870. To celebrate the event, the building committee provided 300 children of the village, aged 5-14, with tea and cake. Men were provided with a pint of beer and women with half a pint.

A "Certificated Master," Mr. Orlando Pearce, was appointed to direct "the instruction of children of the Middle and Labouring classes of Saundersfoot." Initially the curriculum was restricted to Reading, Writing, Spelling, Arithmetic and Scripture. Needlework was also provided for the girls. Later, when properly established, Geography, History, Grammar, English and Drawing were to be introduced. Children below the first standard were charged 1d per week, first, second and third standards 2d per week, and those in the fourth, fifth and sixth standards 3d a week, payable in advance each Monday morning.

The rules of the school reflected the Victorian emphasis on order and discipline. They were extensive and detailed and included : To attend school with hands and faces clean and hair neatly combed. To be promptly obedient to orders without impertinence. Not to throw stones, sticks or mud on, or near, the school premises. Broken panes to be paid for. Not to ink, pencil mark or tear any of the school's books, pictures, placards or maps, or turn down the corners of books. Any article wilfully damaged to be paid for. Not to cut names or marks in the woodwork, nor stand on the forms and seats. No knife to be used — pencils to be pointed before school begins.

During the first week 90 children reported for tuition. Discipline remained a problem, however, because a new master, George Parsons, was appointed after less than two years. He insisted on spending the whole of the first week "teaching discipline." In his second week he complained that, "The children were too lazy to use the closets but were committing nuisances in the playground — girls as well as boys." He also found that George Lewis, a teenage monitor, was receiving "bribes" not to punish the younger pupils and he was dismissed. As the number on role grew two new monitors were appointed to assist the Master. They were both aged 13, and were paid a shilling a week!

The school still stands at the bottom of the Ridgeway, opposite the modern St. Bride's Catholic Church.

Extracted from "The Story of Saundersfoot," by T. G. Stickings.

water. It houses the Sailing Club, which organises a busy summer programme and has a wide, easily used launching slipway for boat owners. Boat fishing from the harbour is varied and specialised tope fishing trips are available. Fresh fish — caught mainly in Saundersfoot Bay — can be purchased from the harbourside stall. There is a large adjacent car park.

Beaches

The village has three excellent sandy beaches, all completely safe for swimming and related activities. To the East of the main village beach lies Coppet Hall Beach, with its easily accessible car park. (Coppet Hall is probably a contraction of "Coal Pit Haul".) To the South West lies the Glen Beach, a pretty sandy cove dotted with rocks and clear rock pools, flanked by beautiful cliffs of brown shale and heavily wooded. These cliffs contain the famous Lady Cave Anti-Cline — a national geological monument. All three beaches have the usual range of beach services.

Glen Beach with Monkstone Point in the distance.

Village Beach looking East. © *Alan Shepherd Transparency Library.*

Fishing Boats moored up along the Harbour Wall. © *Alan Shepherd Transparency Library.*

Entrance to Saundersfoot Harbour.

Views

1. The harbour is the focal point of the village, and any boat trip rounding Monkstone Point and proceeding towards St. Catherine"s Island and Caldey will reward the visitor with impressive cliff scenery, rich in bird life.

2. For the more energetic, the cliff path which hugs the edge of the cliffs between Saundersfoot and Tenby, is highly recommended, with outstanding views in all directions.

3. A less strenuous, but most enjoyable walk, is East from Coppet Hall Beach via the coast path through the tunnels to the pretty sandy cove of Wiseman's Bridge — peaceful now, but formerly used as a training ground during the preparations for the "D-Day landings".

4. St. Issell's Church — set in a wooded valley on the outskirts of the village — is also worth a visit. Take the public footpath through the lovely meadow from Coppet Hall Beach.

SHIPBUILDING IN SAUNDERSFOOT

Two shipbuilding yards were established in Saundersfoot during the 19th century — Beddoes and Reids. Both were situated in what used to be called Railway Street — now The Strand. There were also construction and slipway facilites in the area of the harbour, now occupied by the Saundersfoot Sailing Club dinghy park. Both yards relied heavily on timber cut from the local woods and seasoned on site. When Francis Beddoe died in 1873, H. L. Reid took over his business. These yards specialised in building and repairing small coasting vessels up to a few hundred tons. In later years, Reid's yard derived much of its revenue from general repairs and maintenance work on the sturdy little colliers which called regularly at Saundersfoot to load anthracite from the local coalfield.

Two of the most famous ships to emerge from these yards were the "Verbena" and the "Francis Beddoes." The "Verbena," owned and skippered by Captain Graham, was an elegant 93 ton ketch — over 70 ft. in length with a 20 ft. beam. The "Francis Beddoes" was the first ship built after the amalgamation of the two yards. Launched in 1877, she gave magnificent service around this dangerous coastline for nearly 50 years before going aground in fog on Pendine Sands.

Although not built in Saundersfoot, the "Lady of the Isles" was a ship which engendered great affection in all who knew her. Built in Jersey (hence her name), she weighed 44 tons and was gracefully proportioned. Brought to Saundersfoot by H. L. Reid she became a familiar sight plying between ports all over the Bristol Channel — including fortnightly trips to Bristol. During her last years in Saundersfoot, she was owned and skippered by John Davies — known to the locals as "Captain Jack." She ended her days in Devon. Reid's yard closed in 1910.

St. Issell's Church. © A.S.T.L.

Saundersfoot Village from the Harbour. © A.S.T.L.

Entrance to Hean Castle in Autumn Sunshine
© A.S.T.L.

Pleasant Valley, near Saundersfoot, is a lush, steep-sided valley of small fields, sheltered by fine bands of trees, its floor bisected by a busy stream. The whole valley is open to the South and is sunny and warm. It meets the coast at the popular village of Wiseman's Bridge, where the stream tumbles to the sea over a bank of pebbles. Surveying this peaceful scene today, it is hard to imagine that, less than 130 years ago, the upper reaches of this valley would have echoed to the roar of a blast furnace, the clatter of colliery trucks, and that the air would have been tinged with sulphur, smoke and dust.

Kilgetty Ironworks was built at Stepaside in 1848, because all the raw materials needed — iron ore, coal and limestone were to hand locally. Iron ore was dug from the "levels" along the sea coast between Saundersfoot and Amroth. Groups of these levels were known as "patches". In these patches, using picks and shovels, miners dug the rust brown ore from the cliff faces in areas where the seams of ore outcropped. Piles of the ore would be stored above the high tide mark on the beaches, or at the foot of the cliffs, where it could be washed by the elements, and sorted — often by women and children. Women, known as "pollers" were employed to sort through these piles, selecting the best ore for use in the furnaces. They were equipped with small pointed hammers to test the ore and chip off the shale. Between Coppet Hall and Wiseman's Bridge there were six small ironstone "patches", while between Wiseman's Bridge and Amroth there were four major patches, known locally as Bridge, Lloyds, Crickdam and Burrows. Levels and small shafts for obtaining the

valuable ore were also developed at various localities inland, e.g. Kilvelgy Iron Mine, near Kilgetty. The "patch girls" who worked with the men were "Hardy and exposed to all kinds of weather", and led an almost half-savage life. "They work as hard as the men from whom they differ but little in dress and quite equal in grossness." (R. H. Franks, 1842). The metallic content of the ore dug from these cliffs ranged from 16%-39%.

Limestone, which was essential for the smelting process, was available just three miles to the north from quarries at Ludchurch and Blaencilgoed. Top quality anthracite coal was already mined just a little higher up the valley at Kilgetty and Lower Level collieries.

Kilgetty Ironworks, Stepaside

In 1845 a group of local colliery owners and businessmen commissioned a report by Messrs. M. & F. Foster to "Make proposals to open out this mineral district." As a result, the Pembrokeshire Iron and Coal Company was established on July 18th, 1847, with offices in Saundersfoot and Blackfriars, London. They decided to build their new ironworks at Stepaside. Not only were all the minerals to hand, but the iron produced could easily be transported to the harbour at Saundersfoot, via the narrow gauge railway which had been built in 1840 to service the collieries around Stepaside. The first stone of these new works was laid in August 1848 by Mrs. Vickerman, amidst much speech making, celebratory dinners and firing of cannon. Hopes were high in the local community for many hundreds of desperately needed jobs and the regular wages which went with them. By January 1849, two of the four planned blast furnaces were completed, and one was "fired up". However, before the year was out serious problems arose on all sides. Against a background of severe economic recession and falling prices, shareholder and management problems surfaced. It was, reluctantly, decided not to bring the second furnace into commission. In January, 1850, a gas explosion put the only furnace operating out of action. Repairs were quickly instituted but, because of adverse market conditions, the company did not re-fire the furnace, concentrating instead on its more profitable coal-mining operations. Iron making re-started in 1852, reaching a peak in December of that year when 1,231 tons of iron mine were produced, then fell rapidly, to cease altogether in September 1853. The company again transferred its attention to its coal mining operations, and over the next few years opened several new pits, e.g. Grove Colliery, just above the ironworks, in September 1856.

In 1857, on the recommendation of a Mr. Tregelles, formerly of the Neath Abbey Ironworks, the directors rashly decided to recommence ironmaking at the Kilgetty works with just one furnace. Only 18 months later this damaging "stop-go" cycle was again repeated. Demand for iron was sluggish and, as a result, the men were forced to take a 10% cut in their wages. This led to industrial problems and to a protest meeting on Kingsmoor Common. Matters were further complicated in 1857 when Lord Milford, the landlord of the estate, died and his half-brother, Rev. J. Philipps, succeeded him. This heralded an unpleasant period of prolonged wrangling between Ranken Vickerman, on behalf of the company, and the new landord, over rents and mineral royalties payable. However, despite all the difficulties, this period of ironmaking extended into 1861. In that year, 4,683 tons of iron were shipped out of Saundersfoot. This included 1,522 tons sent to Port Talbot, now one of the great steel producing centres of Europe.

By 1862 the ill-fated works was at a standstill once more, and the furnaces stood cold and silent for the third time since the works opened in 1849. Ranken Vickerman now became the sole owner. Ever optimistic, and determined to make the project succeed, perhaps with one eye on the coming of the Pembroke and Tenby railway, he rebuilt and enlarged one furnace which was back in blast before the end of 1863. The works lurched on from crisis to crisis, but by January 1868 it was again closed. In 1872 it was still closed and Vickerman decided that the time had finally come to sell. James Carlton of Knutsford, Cheshire, agreed to purchase the Railway and Harbour Company, Bonvilles

Court Colliery and the Kilgetty Collieries and Ironworks in June 1872 for an agreed price of £144,140. Vickerman still retained some shares in the new company which was called Bonvilles Court Coal and Iron Company, founded in May, 1873. Investment was made available for the railway, and on May 29th, the Tenby Observer reported that "great preparations are being made at Kilgetty Ironworks which are intended to be put into blast early next week." Yet another attempt was to be made to salvage the works from extinction, but this time the end would be quick and final. Another bout of countrywide economic recession and falling prices led the management to impose an immediate cut of 10% in the colliers' wages. This led, predictably, to walk-outs and a short strike. Thirteen days later, when the colliers returned to work, having accepted a 5% cut in wages, the furnace in the ironworks had been extinguished, never to be relit.

Bonvilles Court Coal and Iron Company struggled on against growing problems and industrial unrest until 1877, when action by the company's creditors led to the appointment of a receiver. However, the receiver continued to run the colliery business. On 17th May, 1878, in Tenby, the entire property and plant of the Bonvilles Court Coal and Iron Co. were offered for sale by auction. The only bidder was the company's largest creditor, Ranken Vickerman, who was owed over £100,000 from the sale to James Carlton. In view of his involvement the liquidator and the court, accepted an offer of just £10,000 for the lot. Vickerman, thus, regained control of the company and the benefit of capital investment from 1873, estimated at between £40,000-£50,000, for a "bargain basement" price. In 1882 he made a detailed study of converting Kilgetty Ironworks to the new Bessemer process, but this time nothing came of his efforts. In 1887 and 1888 the machinery was dismantled and removed. The large stack on the hillside above the furnace was demolished in 1909. In the 39 years that the ironworks was on the site and capable of production, it actually produced pig-iron for a total of only twelve. A chequered history indeed!

A few years ago the Stepaside Industrial Heritage Trust was established, and interest in this facet of South Pembrokeshire's history was re-kindled. The project is well worth a visit. Here you can see the remains of the Ironworks and related industrial activity. The Interpretative Centre has a wealth of interesting material to stir your imagination and breathe fire and life into these powerful industrial relics.

Location — follow the signs from Kilgetty By-Pass. See also walks 2 and 3 on pages 135-140 which provide many more details on the coal and iron industry of South Pembrokeshire.

Pembroke

Henry VII, born at Pembroke Castle in 1457.

The ancient town of Pembroke is an excellent touring centre for South Pembrokeshire. Car parking is readily available and there is a wide range of accommodation of all sorts with the accompanying range of interesting shops and restaurants.

Pembroke was formerly the county town, before Haverfordwest grew in importance and assumed the role in the 16th Century. Dominating the main street is the massive, well preserved Norman Castle which boasts the finest Keep of all the Welsh Castles. The original castle was built of "stakes" and "turf" on the superb site of a limestone ridge, largely surrounded by water and marshes. The Normans quickly realised its central strategic importance in colonising the South of the county and the first stone castle was built in 1105 by Gerald of Windsor. However, the present castle was mainly the work of William Marshall and his five sons during the years 1189-1245. The town itself was fortified and walled and sections of these walls are still visible from the one-way traffic system on the southern side of the town and from the Mill Pond Walk to the north. For the next 300

Pembroke Castle, 1817. From a Watercolour by Charles Norris.

Clock Tower, Main Street. © *A.S.T.L.*

Part of the Old Town Wall, Pembroke

Top Right: The Mill Pond, Pembroke. © *A.S.T.L.*

years the castle was the home of the Earls of Pembroke and was instrumental in the pacification and reorganisation of "Little England Beyond Wales" on the clear lines of the Norman Feudal System. Henry VII was born here in 1457 and his family retained close ties with the castle during and after his reign. During the turbulent years of the Civil War, the castle was attacked in turn by both the Royalists and the Roundheads, and during the later stages of the struggle the attacking force was led by Cromwell himself. The castle held out courageously for 48 days — the keep in particular was pounded by cannons for six weeks without serious effect, until Cromwell finally ran out of cannon balls and was forced to make do with beach pebbles! Mayor Poyer, one of the leaders of the revolt against Parliament,

THE SOUTH PEMBROKESHIRE DIALECT

The South Pembrokeshire Dialect is quite unique. It has arisen out of a combination of the county's remoteness, its seafaring links with Ireland and the West of England and, most importantly, from its rich history of invasion, conquest, settlement and inter-marriage. Even before the Norman colonisation of the south of the county, this area had already been invaded by Saxons, Irish and Norsemen. With the arrival of the Normans in the 11th century, English replaced Welsh as the language of the home. Later, large numbers of Flemings settled in the area. All of these factors have resulted in the diverse and individual nature of the dialect of "down below," as South Pembrokeshire is often referred to by the more Celtic North of the county.

Baste/Lambaste	— *To thrash, flog, beat soundly*
Bessy	— *A man who interferes too much in domestic affairs*
Caffle	— *Tangle*
Tamping	— *Very angry*
Skew-whiff	— *On the slant*
Traipse	— *To plod/wander aimlessly*
Kift	— *Awkward, clumsy*
Sprag	— *Skid*
Drang	— *Narrow passage between two walls*
Fail	— *To be unable to finish a meal*
Heck	— *To hop on one leg*
Moil	— *To root in the ground like a pig*
Old Boy	— *A batchelor*
Pile	— *Throw*
Rab	— *Broken stone*
Scaddly	— *Greedy, destructive*
Now just	— *A little while ago*
Frit	— *A small person or thing*

47

In 1456, Margaret Beaufort, Countess of Richmond was staying at Pembroke Castle under the protection of her uncle, Jasper Tudor. She was 15 years old and pregnant. Her husband Edmund Tudor, Earl of Richmond, was away fighting for the Lancastrians in the War of the Roses. Later that year, Edmund returned to his young bride — but tragically died at Carmarthen in November. Just weeks later, on 28th January, 1457, Margaret gave birth to a healthy son — Henry — later to become Henry VII, founder of the Tudor dynasty. Although there is some uncertainty about the exact place of his birth, it probably occurred in one of the first floor rooms in the tower to the south west of the gatehouse.

Henry Richmond spent most of his carefree childhood years at the castle exploring its nooks and crannies and playing by the nearby Pembroke River which lapped the castle walls. His relationship with his mother was particularly close and she ensured that he received a well balanced education and grew to enjoy books and appreciate music. In 1471, when he was 14, the castle was besieged by an army of renegade Welshmen, led by the rebellious brother of Sir Rhys ap Thomas (see p. 96). Henry escaped through one of the secret entrances and with his mother and uncle Jasper they fled to Tenby. Days later they were smuggled on to a small coastal schooner lying in the harbour to make their escape first to the Channel Islands and then to Brittany.

In Brittany, to the growing concern of the Yorkists who tried to get the family "extradited," Henry became an increasingly influential figure amongst the dissident groups. Plans were soon afoot for Henry to return to Britain to claim the throne as the true heir to the House of Lancaster. Fourteen years after his enforced exile he landed at Dale on 7th August, 1485, at the head of a small but enthusiastic army. Raising the banners of St. George and Cadwallader against the "unnatural tyrant," they were immediately joined by the most powerful nobleman in Wales — Sir Rhys ap Thomas of Carew Castle. Sir Rhys provided a large number of men of arms and put much of his personal wealth at Henry's disposal. Marching eastwards through Wales, the justness of his cause proclaimed by the Welsh bards, he provided a rallying point for all the anti-Yorkist factions.

By the time they reached Bosworth for the decisive battle against the army of Richard III, Henry rode at the head of over 5,000 men. Desperately betrayed and deserted by some of his more politically astute commanders at the last minute, Richard was dragged from his horse and died fighting valiantly.

Henry Tudor's son, Henry VIII later gifted Pembroke Castle to the beautiful young Anne Boleyn, creating her Marchioness of Pembroke in 1532. Four years later, after his marriage had been annulled, he abolished the Palatinate and Pembroke reverted to crown property.

was taken to London shortly afterwards and shot at Covent Garden. The mill bridge, which now carries the main road to Pembroke Dock, used to contain a large water-driven corn mill, which burned down in the late 1930's. The adjacent quays reflect Pembroke's past importance as a sea port, which reached its zenith in 1750 when it was the premier port of South Wales. The quays then bustled with tall ships bringing cargoes of wine, salt, cloth, timber and loading with wool, hides, salted butter and herrings in barrrels.

After a stroll down the main street, flanked with a good selection of shops, relax for a while on one of the seats along the attractive Mill Pond Walk. The children will enjoy the swans and ducks — especially if you have some bread to feed them. Nearby Monkton Priory, built in 1098 for the Benedictine Order, abandoned at the reformation, then restored in the 19th century, is also worth a visit.

View over the Battlements to the Mill Bridge and Mill Pond.

Pembroke Castle.

49

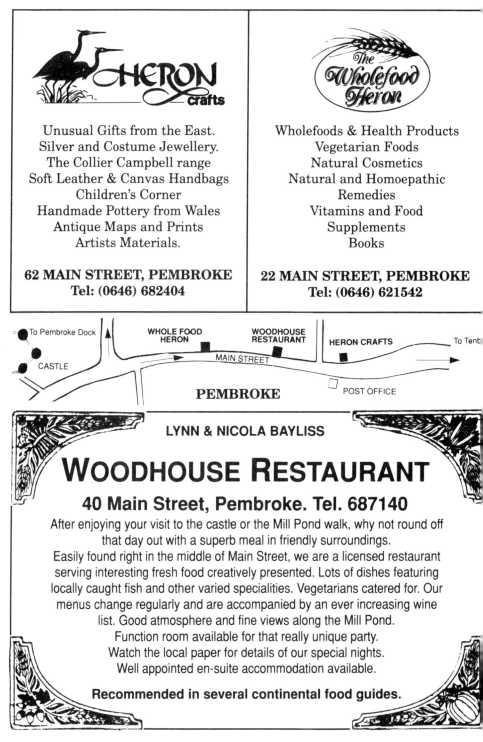

The magnificent Circular Keep, Pembroke Castle.   © *Alan Shepherd Transparency Library*

The Gatehouse, Pembroke Castle.   © *Alan Shepherd Transparency Library*

51

Around the Pembrokeshire Coast

This next major section of the Guide deals in detail with the entire Pembrokeshire coastline from Laugharne in the South East to Cardigan in the North East. Every coastal village and its associated beach or cove is described and particular care has been taken to include those lovely remote beaches which, without local knowledge, remain largely hidden away. Throughout this survey of some of the most exhilarating coastline in Britain, reference is made to particularly dramatic viewpoints. This will allow those, whose freedom of movement may be limited by age or infirmity, or because of wet weather, to enjoy what many seasoned travellers agree is a coastline without equal.

* Laugharne, Pendine and Marros lie just over the county border in Carmarthenshire.

Part one:
The South Coast
Laugharne to Angle

Laugharne

A quiet, pretty town beside the estuary of the

Dylan's Writing Shed — "The Water and Tree Room".
© Alan Shepherd Transparency Library.

River Taf, most famous in recent years for the "Boathouse" home of the poet Dylan Thomas, who is buried in the churchyard of the 13th Century church. King Street refers to the visit of Henry II on his return from an expedition to Ireland. Ruined castle, pleasant riverside walks rich in bird life and interesting cobbled lanes and Georgian architecture. See p131 for details of the Dylan Thomas Boathouse.

See p131 for details of the Dylan Thomas Boathouse.

Nature Trail *Sir John's Hill Nature trail leaflet — West Wales Naturalist's Trust, available from local shops.*

Laugharne Castle.   *© Alan Shepherd Transparency Library*

South Pembrokeshire - Towns - Villages - Beaches - Views

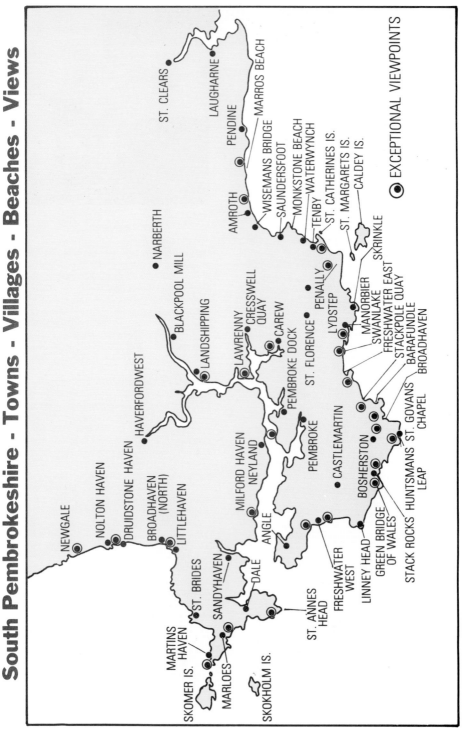

EXCEPTIONAL VIEWPOINTS

ST. CLEARS
LAUGHARNE
MARROS BEACH
PENDINE
AMROTH
WISEMANS BRIDGE
SAUNDERSFOOT
MONKSTONE BEACH
WATERWYNCH
TENBY
ST. CATHERINES IS.
ST. MARGARETS IS.
CALDEY IS.
SKRINKLE
NARBERTH
BLACKPOOL MILL
CRESSWELL QUAY
PENALLY
LYDSTEP
MANORBIER
SWANLAKE
FRESHWATER EAST
STACKPOLE QUAY
BARAFUNDLE
BROADHAVEN
LAWRENNY
CAREW
ST. FLORENCE
LANDSHIPPING
HAVERFORDWEST
PEMBROKE DOCK
MILFORD HAVEN
NEYLAND
ANGLE
PEMBROKE
CASTLEMARTIN
BOSHERSTON
ST. GOVANS CHAPEL
NEWGALE
NOLTON HAVEN
DRUIDSTONE HAVEN
BROADHAVEN (NORTH)
LITTLEHAVEN
DALE
GREEN BRIDGE OF WALES
HUNTSMANS LEAP
STACK ROCKS
ST. BRIDES
SANDYHAVEN
FRESHWATER WEST
LINNEY HEAD
ST. ANNES HEAD
MARTINS HAVEN
MARLOES
SKOMER IS.
SKOKHOLM IS.

53

DYLAN THOMAS

Dylan working on the wall of the Boathouse garden.

The Boathouse. © A.S.T.L.

Dylan Thomas was born in Swansea and educated at the local Grammar School. He left Wales in 1934 for "Smokey London paved with poems." Following his marriage to Caitlin in 1937, they arrived in Laugharne and set up home in a dilapidated cottage in Gosport Street. In 1939, now with their first child, they moved to "Sea View," a comfortable home adjoining the grounds of Laugharne Castle. The castle at this time was rented by another writer, Richard Hughes, who allowed Dylan to use the gazebo in the castle walls to write in. Here Dylan wrote "Portrait of the Artist as a Young Dog." However, severe financial problems led them to sell all their furniture and leave Laugharne. During the war, Dylan eked out a living by writing film scripts, but by 1945 the family was living in abject poverty and largely dependent on the generosity of friends. The family spent a year in Oxford, living in a one-roomed summer chalet in the garden of the historian A.J.P. Taylor and his wife Margaret, one of Dylan's most loyal patrons.

In 1948 "The Boathouse" came on to the market, and Dylan heard of the coming sale. Desperate to return to Wales, he wrote a series of moving letters to the Taylors, and to his eternal gratitude Margaret Taylor bought the house for £2,500. After arranging for water and electricity to be installed, the Thomas family moved in May, 1949. Dylan's parents also moved into a cottage in King Street, Laugharne, called "The Pelican." This was conveniently situated opposite his favourite hostelry — "Browns Hotel." Dylan converted the garage and cycle shed into a study, away from the noise of the family. He was extremely happy and wrote to Margaret Taylor:-

"All I shall write in this water and tree room on the cliff, every word of it will be in thanks to you . . . you have given me my life and now I am going to live it."

The next few months were amongst his most productive, and he made good progress on his best known work "Under Milk Wood" and several poems. Caitlin set about making the Boathouse into their first real home, and the outlook for the Thomases and their children, Llewellyn, Aeronwy and Colm appeared quite bright.

Before long, however, financial problems began to surface and Dylan decided to undertake a reading tour of his work in America. This was an immediate success. With this success came additional pressure and careful scrutiny by the Inland Revenue, which resulted in yet more complications with family liquidity. During the next four years he produced much of his finest work in "the shack" above the estuary. However, growing public recognition produced further personal problems and an ever increasing consumption of alcohol. This was especially so during the, by now annual, American tours, when he was away from family and friends and was the guest at endless literary parties where his drinking reached dangerous levels.

On 9th November, 1953, Dylan collapsed and died on a lecture trip to New York. His body was returned to his beloved Laugharne — "This timeless, mild, beguiling island of a town"— to be buried in the annexe to the churchyard on 24th November, the grave now marked by a simple white, wooden cross.

Caitlin Thomas sold the Boathouse in 1973 to a trust established to turn the property into a memorial to Dylan. It is now owned by the Carmarthenshire District Council.

Those planning to visit Dylan Thomas's home should purchase a copy of "The Boathouse Laugharne" by Lorraine Scourfield. This concise and well illustrated guide is available from the boathouse and from good bookshops throughout West Wales.

Pendine

A small village nestling at the Western end of the vast expanse of Pendine Sands — the venue of many world land speed record attempts in the 1920's (see insert). A large part of the beach is now used by the M.O.D. as an experimental rocket and artillery range. Vehicles may be taken on to the beach and boats launched from the slipway and from the beach. Good holiday facilities in the village. For those with a special interest in motor sport, drop in to the Beach Hotel — used as the base for many of the world land speed record attempts. Here you will find a superb collection of fascinating old photographs lining the walls, and the beer is good as well.

Marros

A fine, long sandy beach, usually deserted because of its difficult access, which is on foot, via a rough lane from Marros Village on the main Pendine-Amroth road. Desert island atmosphere accentuated especially in wintertime by piles of driftwood and other flotsam which is often washed up after a storm. At low water spring tides, ebonized tree stumps and small banks of peat — part of the remains of a prehistoric sunken forest — are visible on certain parts of the beach. Well worth the plod down the 400 ft. high grassy banks which buttress the beach. Note the old hill fort at "Top Castle" above the wooded valley at the

---

PENDINE SANDS AND THE WORLD LAND SPEED RECORD

On the sands between 1924 and 1927 the world land speed record was broken five times:

1924.	Malcolm Campbell	Sunbeam
	146.16 m.p.h.	
1926.	Malcolm Campbell	Sunbeam
	150.87 m.p.h.	
1926.	J.G.P. Thomas	Thomas (Babs)
	169.30 m.p.h.	
1926.	J.G.P. Thomas	Thomas (Babs)
	171.02 m.p.h.	
1927.	Malcolm Campbell	Napier Campbell
	174.224 m.p.h.	

Western end of the beach. No facilities, so pack that rucksack and have a day away from it all.

Telpyn Cove

At low water and half tide, Telpyn is simply an extension of the Eastern end of Amroth Beach, past the stream which flows across the beach at New Inn. However, at high water the cove must be reached by the public footpath from the Pendine-Amroth road, some 300 yards below the entrance to Telpyn Riding

Pendine Beach looking towards Gilman Point.   © *Alan Shepherd Transparency Library.*

Marros Beach.   © *A.S.T.L.*

Stables. No sand at high water, pebbles and large flat rocks to sunbathe on. Warm and sheltered.

Amroth

Pleasant village with excellent sandy beach backed by groynes and pebbles. Inns, Cafés, Accommodation, shops and a launching slip to the beach. Exposed to Easterly winds — several houses lying to the seaward side of the road through the village were washed away during storms earlier this century. At very low tide remains of an ancient sunken forest may be visible. Amroth marks the Eastern end of the 167 mile long Pembrokeshire Coast footpath, and the stream next to the New Inn forms the Eastern boundary of the old county of Pembrokeshire.

Amroth Castle, now a hotel and caravan site, is a 19th century house built on the site of a much earlier castle. In 1802, Admiral Lord Nelson visited Pembrokeshire with Sir William Hamilton and his wife Emma, and they lunched at the castle with Captain Ackland, the owner. On hearing Nelson's great victory, and subsequent death at Trafalgar, Captain Ackland inserted a commemorative plaque into the ceiling of the drawing room in the Castle, where it remains today.

Wiseman's Bridge

A picturesque little beach at the end of the

The huge sweep of Amroth Beach from the East.   © *Alan Shepherd Transparency Library.*

Captain Malcolm Campbell at Pendine, 1926.

Record attempts at Pendine were always better attempted during the winter months. The cooler conditions suited the high performance racing engines, and the winter surf pounded the surface of the beach into a smoother, if often wetter racing platform.

In 1927 Malcolm Campbell returned to Pembrokeshire with his re-designed "Bluebird" car, now powered by an enormous 500 HP Napier Aero engine. Atrocious weather with heavy rain and high winds interfered with tuning sessions and essential practice runs, and some of the less enthusiastic members of the press corps quietly excused themselves and slipped back to their more comfortable offices. A frustrated Campbell was often seen pacing the beach, looking forlornly at the sombre, rain-swept sky.

Eventually the weather did break and helped by the new technique of ploughing the sand alongside the "track", the beach began to dry quickly. After some hectic practice sessions, February 4th was assigned as the day for the attempt and all necessary arrangements made with timekeepers and official scrutineers. By the time the huge car was wheeled down the ramp onto the beach, the track was already marked with flags by the loyal band of helpers and the beach was drying nicely as the tide receded. Several hundred people had gathered on the beach and they stood talking excitedly in small groups, their backs turned against the chill wind which once again was driving ominous grey clouds in over Carmarthen Bay. They

were not to be disappointed this time. As the time approached, conversation fell away and eyes glanced nervously back up the beach towards Pendine — Campbell was on his way. The crowd watched mesmerised as the distant black spot and its whining trail of sound appeared to be propelled down the beach by some superhuman force. Within seconds it was alongside the measured mile. Campbell's taut, helmetted figure was now plainly visible in this pale blue projectile which devoured the beach with a shattering roar as its huge engine now strained at full throttle. Then it was gone, bathing the spectators in a swirling cloud of salt spray and blue exhaust, their faces peppered with angry particles of sand.

When the second run had been completed, jubilation greeted the news that the mean speed achieved was 174.224 miles per hour. Malcolm Campbell was once again the fastest man on earth on four wheels.

*Campbell later revealed that the attempt had nearly ended in disaster when on the return run the wind had torn off his goggles and he had been temporarily blinded by the stinging sand and salt spray.

Just one month later, on Thursday, 3rd March, 41-year-old Parry Thomas, driving "Babs", was killed at Pendine, trying to smash Malcolm Campbell's newly established record. In a grisly accident, the top of his head was completely removed by the broken drive chain of his car. No further land speed records were broken at Pendine. Higher speeds dictated less troublesome racing surfaces, and yet more space to accelerate to the higher terminal speeds subsequently achieved.

Wiseman's Bridge Beach.   © *Alan Shepherd Transparency Library.*

Clifftop view of Monkstone Beach.   © *Alan Shepherd Transparency Library.*

THE WRECK OF THE TREVIGA

For centuries Marros and Pendine beaches have had fearsome reputations as graveyards for sailing ships. Unfortunate vessels found themselves trying to claw to windward into the teeth of westerly gales, while all the time being driven ever closer to the mountainous surf which pounded these vast open beaches. Many of the older houses in Pendine were built from timber salvaged from these wrecks, whose cargoes and fittings provided a morbid bounty for the coastal communities. Tales also abound of unscrupulous locals who worked with the elements to lure ships to destruction on this lee shore.

One of the last large vessels to be wrecked on these sands was the Russian schooner, the Treviga. Returning, in 1923, from Trinidad with a cargo of pitch, she was running before a full westerly gale with reduced sail when she approached the Welsh coast, bound for Cardiff. Prudently, the master ran for shelter to Caldey Roads. Here he turned down an offer from the Saundersfoot Pilot, Mr. Jack Childs, to bring the ship into the safety of Tenby Harbour. Instead, Captain Jacobson elected to save money and ride the storm out at anchor. During the night the wind veered, increased in strength and the anchor began to drag. Tenby lifeboat was summoned, and in atrocious conditions the crew showed great seamanship to manoeuvre alongside and rescue the entire crew of seven, the master and his wife. The stricken ship narrowly missed the Woolhouse Rocks off Tenby before being driven across the bay to her doom at Morfabychan, between Marros and Pendine. The following day a chastened Capt. Jacobson arrived above the cove to ascertain the fate of his ship and her cargo. He was met by a woman coming up the path, resplendent in his wife's fur coat! The villagers had already claimed another harvest from the sea.

wooded "Pleasant Valley". Used as a practice location for the Normandy landings in 1944 when the manoeuvres were watched by Churchill and Mountbatten. Pretty wooded walk up the aptly named "Pleasant Valley" to see the remains of the old Kilgetty Ironworks, which was supplied with ore dug locally from "patches" on the nearby cliffs. Conveniently situated Inn and Shop just above high water mark!

Named after the Wyseman family who had extensive lands in the Wiseman's Bridge/Sardis area. Thomas Wyseman Mayor of Tenby 1403, was of the same family.

Two detailed walks through much of the recent history of this fascinating locality are described on pages 135-140.

Monkstone

Glorious sandy beach to the South of the narrow finger of Monkstone Point. Access is by footpath only, steep in places, from the cliffpath between Saundersfoot and Tenby, and by road access via Trevayne Farm. Some limited parking in farm lane. No facilities. Best visited in morning and early afternoon. Treat the cliffs with great caution — high and steep with loose shale — NOT suitable for climbing. Called Monkstone because there is the remains of a monastic cell on the point itself. The name first appears on Saxtons map of 1578.

Sea Pinks © *A.S.T.L.*

Waterwych Bay. © *A.S.T.L.*

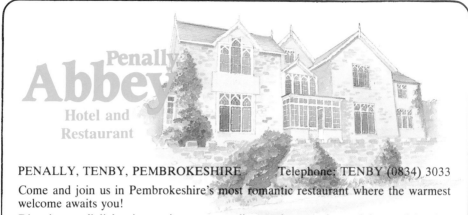

Penally Abbey
Hotel and Restaurant

PENALLY, TENBY, PEMBROKESHIRE   Telephone: TENBY (0834) 3033

Come and join us in Pembrokeshire's most romantic restaurant where the warmest welcome awaits you!

Dine by candlelight, in gracious surroundings, where each meal is a celebration especially prepared for you.

Enjoy mouthwatering dishes of fresh seasonal delicacies, complimented by excellent wines from our cellar.

Better still, spend the night in one of our four poster beds. Enjoy a late, late breakfast. We KNOW how important you are and aim to make your stay memorable.

Open all Year   Major Credit Cards Accepted

To avoid disappointment please phone for your Dinner Reservations
Tenby (0834) 3033

View along the South Beach towards Tenby, from Giltar Point, Penally. © Alan Shepherd Transparency Library.

Lydstep Haven with Caldey Island in the background. © *Alan Shepherd Transparency Library*

Waterwynch

Delightful, small, sandy cove set in a rocky cleft in the cliffs between Tenby and Monkstone Point. At low water, plenty of rock pools and neighbouring caves to explore, but watch for the incoming tide. Access from the Tenby-Saundersfoot road (A478) or by foot from coast path. No car park at the beach. Best visited in mornings or early afternoon. As the name implies, Waterwynch was the site of an old water mill used for grinding locally grown corn. The present house was built by the local artist Charles Norris, on land given to him by Tenby Corporation. Many of Norris's paintings are on exhibition at Tenby Museum.

Penally

A pleasant sunny and well kept village, built largely in the lee of the Ridgeway, overlooking the burrows and Tenby Golf Course. Interesting church — St. Teilo's with the remains of a 6th Century Celtic Cross. Good village facilities. Spectacular views from above the village over the cliffs at Giltar Point and on to Caldey and St Margaret's, and on a clear day as far as Lundy Island. Ask in the village for "Strawberry Lane" and proceed with caution up to the Ridgeway. One mile away is Hoyles Mouth Cave, an important archaeological site. Car parking in the Station Yard, off the bye-pass,

and also round the village green, opposite the craft shop and pottery.

The footpath from the station car park to the South Beach cuts across the railway line, the army firing range and Tenby Golf Course. Although not as dangerous as may first appear (!), visitors are asked to keep a 'weather eye open' where the path cuts directly across the line of the 9th tee. Golfing tempers understandably get a little frayed when their game is held up while picnic parties are moved on!!

Nature Trail *Penally Nature Trail, produced by the Friends of Penally — available in Village Shop.*

Lystep Haven

Private estate with admission charge. Truly beautiful cove with lovely coastal scenery and views towards Caldey Island. Lydstep headland, to the West of the bay, was used for quarrying limestone, and the sloops and schooners were loaded directly from the cliffs, weather conditions permitting. The large house overlooking the beach, which now forms the administrative offices of the estate, was built by Viscount St. David's at the end of the 19th Century. The headland was presented to the National trust in 1936 by the Pilgrim Trust. It may be reached via the footpath from the estate, or from the National Trust Car Park.

View over Saddle Rock to Lydstep Bay. © *A.S.T.L.*

Lydstep Caverns.   © *A.S.T.L.*

Lydstep Village and the Cavern's Beach

Much of the village was built by the first Viscount St. David's in the 19th Century. The old building adjacent to the Village Post Office and Stores is the Palace of Arms, described as the hunting seat of Bishop Gower of St. David's (1328-47). It may have been used as an armour house.

Some 70 yards on, past the Lydstep tavern, turn left and after half mile locate the Lydstep Headland Car Park. You are now conveniently situated: (a) for exploring the magnificent headland; (b) for climbing down the steep, but well made path to the low water caverns beach. This is an attractive sandy beach with plenty of rock pools, and of course the interesting and very large caverns to explore. No facilities of any kind, so be prepared to bring a snack with you.

Skrinkle Beach

Until recently, this beach was part of the M.O.D. base at Manorbier, and was not open to the public. Magnificent little beach, surrounded by very high cliffs, particularly well sheltered from all Westerly winds. Very fine sand and clear water. No facilities, apart from a small car park, but highly recommended, though the climb down the steps to the beach is quite arduous — not for the elderly or the infirm.

Location: When approaching Manorbier from the direction of Tenby turn left into the old army camp married quarters (approx. half a mile to the East of Manorbier), then follow the signs. For those unable to make the descent to this splendid little beach, by-pass the first car park on your right, which serves the beach only, and drive on for another half mile to the second car park near the clifftop. This overlooks a glorious stretch of cliffs running eastwards to the Caverns Beach at Lydstep, with St. Margaret's and Caldey in the distance. Here you will find a National Parks picnic site with trestle tables, etc. — when you can tear yourself away from the view the air will work wonders for your appetite.

Precipe Beach

A low water beach only, so use your tide table to plan your visit. **Location:** Drive to Manorbier Village, park in the main Car Park beside the castle. Follow the footpath outlined in Walk 6 p.143 to the point known as Priest's Nose on the Southern flank of the beach, then via the **clifftop path** for another threequarter mile before descending the steep steps to the beach. The beach has no facilities whatsoever, and your only company could well be the sea birds. Notice that the cliffs have now changed to old red sandstone. Old Castle Head at the Eastern end of the beach is the site of an Iron Age Fort, c. 300 B.C.

Manorbier

Original name Maenor Pyr — the manor of Pyr. Later, in the 14th Century it was simply called Beere. A small sandy beach flanked by high cliffs of red sandstone. A tiny freshwater stream flows across the beach and there are some excellent rock pools for the children. Giraldus Cambrensis, a much travelled medieval priest called Manorbier, "the loveliest spot in Wales". The beach is dominated by the ramparts of Manorbier Castle, which is open to the public and enjoys panoramic views over the beach and out into the Bristol Channel. The present owner of the castle, Lady Dunsany, is a descendant of Sir Erasmus Phillips of Picton Castle, who purchased the castle in 1670. The picturesque church built on the opposite side of the valley dates from the 12th Century.

The beach is now a favourite haunt for surfers. Pleasant, compact village with good facilities. Large car park just above beach with toilets. (See p.143 for details of a first class coastal walk from Manorbier.)

Skrinkle Beach, near Manorbier.   © *A.S.T.L.*

Manorbier Beach and Castle   © *Alan Shepherd Transparency Library.*

Manorbier Castle

Entrance to the Castle.

© Alan Shepherd Transparency Library.

The first castle on this spectacular site above Manorbier beach was a simple affair with earth fortifications enclosing crude wooden buildings. The present limestone fortress was built largely by Odo de Barri in the 12th century, though building continued intermittently till around 1300. However, Manorbier was never a fortress such as Pembroke. Essentially it was always a fortified mansion, built to administer and protect its rich and productive farming estate. Within the castle, the great hall was the centre of all activity. On either side were the state apartments where important guests were entertained. Adjacent to the hall was the kitchen and the buttery, and fresh water was available from the nearby well.

The castle's most famous inhabitant was Gerald de Barri — Giraldus Cambrensis — who was born here in 1147. Gerald was the son of William de Barri, a Norman knight, and Angharad, the daughter of a Norman lord and a Welsh princess. He was, thus, directly related to both the new masters of Pembrokeshire's destiny — the Norman aristocracy, and to the old Welsh princes who for years had fought and plotted for control of West Wales. Extremely intelligent and honest he was, thus, ideally placed to steer a balanced and diplomatic course through these turbulent times. Gerald went on to win the loyalty and respect of all who knew him and became one of the greatest scholars that Wales has ever produced. "So long as Wales shall stand by the writings of the Chroniclers, and by the songs of the bards, shall Gerald's noble deeds be praised." — Prince Llewellyn the Great.

Gerald was educated initially at St. David's where his uncle, David Fitzgerald, was bishop, then at Gloucester Abbey and finally at the University of Paris. While his brothers went on to become Norman knights, Gerald became a priest and an authority on the Church in Wales, identifying himself more and more with his Welsh as opposed to his Norman ancestors. He campaigned to become Bishop of St. David's and received much support in this from his Welsh relatives, keen to foster more independence from the Normans. When his uncle died in 1175, Gerald was unanimously elected Bishop of St. David's by the Welsh and English canons of the diocese. However, Henry II was a wily political strategist and recognised the latent threat involved in appointing Gerald to this extremely powerful position, far from London. When the Archbishop of Canterbury interceded on Gerald's behalf, it evoked the following response from Henry — "It is neither necessary or expedient for king or archbishop that a man of great honesty or vigour should become Bishop of St. David's for fear that the crown and Canterbury should suffer thereby." This appointment, Henry continued, would only "Give strength to the Welsh and increase their pride." Subsequently, the king's own choice, a Dutchman, was appointed by the electors of the diocese under threat of losing all their lands if they thwarted the king's wishes.

64

Six years later, Wales was in a state of unrest with minor rebellions continuing against Norman landlords. Henry needed a man of standing with sound Welsh connections and Gerald was sent for. At court he became an advisor on Welsh affairs, and tutor and chaplain to the princes who were to become Richard the Lionheart and King John. In 1198 the Bishop of St. David's died. After bitter political in-fighting, King John accepted Gerald's nomination, and he was again unanimously elected as Bishop of St. David's. He travelled to Rome to be consecrated by the Pope but, once again, political events moved against him. The Archbishop of Canterbury, who Gerald had exposed as being corrupt, stirred up problems and John was persuaded to change his mind. The Vatican vacillated and Gerald's appointment was not consecrated. On his return, court edicts were issued which would have made him guilty of rebellion had he pursued his case.

Gerald is best remembered now for his two books — "Itinerary Through Wales" (1188) and, a little later his "Description Through Wales." Of the seventeen books that he is known to have produced, these two accounts, written in elegant Latin, perhaps best reveal his impressive intellect, keen powers of observation and gentle wit. They provide the most comprehensive contemporary portrait of life in Wales in the latter part of the 12th century available to us. In his "Itinerary Through Wales" in 1188, he described Manorbier thus:-
"The castle in Manorbier is excellently well defended by turrets and bulwarks . . . having on its northern and southern sides a fine fish pond under its walls, as conspicuous for its grand appearance as for the depth of its waters and a beautiful orchard on the same side, enclosed on one part by a vineyard and on the other by a wood, remarkable for the projections of its rocks and the height of its hazel trees."
He died in 1233 and is thought to be buried in his beloved St. David's, though it is possible that he was denied even this.

The last member of the de Barri family to own Manorbier was David, a mysterious personality who used the names David Roche and Edward Barr. He sold the property in the fourteenth century to two separate people and caused such legal mayhem that Henry IV had to step in and granted Manorbier to the Countess of Huntingdon and her husband, Sir John Cornwall. Throughout all its early history, because of the de Barri family links with many of the marauding Welsh princes, the castle escaped serious damage, e.g., during the revolts of Lord Rhys ap Gruffydd and later,

when the huge army of 14,000 Welsh under Owain Glyndwr rampaged through Pembrokeshire. After the Wars of the Roses the castle became crown property and was administered by a series of absentee landlords who displayed little interest in the manor, apart from the revenue it generated. The castle was then sold to the Bowens of Trefloyne (near Tenby). By 1601, the buildings were semi-derelict and the interior of the castle was used for grazing cattle. During the Civil War the castle was prepared for defence against the Parliamentarians. Ditches were dug in front of the gatehouse and windows were modified for use by troops with muskets.

However, General Rowland Laugharne captured the castle with little serious opposition in September 1645, the defenders quickly realising that the siege cannon of the attacking force would soon reduce the old defences to rubble. In 1670 the Bowens sold the property to Sir Erasmus Phillips of Picton Castle, near Haverfordwest, for £6,000. Its present owner, Lady Dunsany, is descended from Sir Erasmus Phillips. The modern residence within the inner ward was built by J.R. Cobb who leased the castle for a period from 1880.

The Gatehouse, Manorbier Castle. © A.S.T.L.

THE KINGS QUOIT — MANORBIER

This impressive Neolithic stone tomb or cromlech is situated beside the coastal footpath leading to the headland known as the Priest's Nose to the south of Manorbier Bay (see map on p. 143). It is one of many such tombs that Neolithic man built in Pembrokeshire (see also Pentre Ifan on p. 93). With a combination of simple technology — rollers and wooden levers — and muscle power in numbers, the cromlech makers managed to manhandle huge stones, often weighing many tons, and then raise them into position. In the King's Quoit the capstone has slewed forward a little as a result of the partial collapse of one of the outer uprights. Originally the tomb would probably have been covered with piles of carefully placed stones, arranged to leave a small opening, giving the completed tomb the appearance of a small cave. Over the centuries these small stones were often removed by farmers to use for walls, farm buildings, etc.

Apart from knowing how they were built, and that they were used for tombs, archaeologists still know comparatively little about the cromlech makers themselves, or about the society they were part of.

Swanlake

A lovely isolated bay between Manorbier and Freshwater East (see map), set amongst high cliffs of red sandstone with rather coarse sand. Safe swimming and lovely clear water. Car parking by permission of the farmers at East Moor and West Moor Farms. Both of these farms are originally Norman Land Grant farms and formed part of the old Lordship of Manorbier. Footpath access from car parks and from coastal footpath. The beach faces due South, so plenty of sunshine. No facilities. * Final descent to the beach is down a high and steep grassy bank — not suitable for the elderly or disabled.

Lamphey

The Bishop's Palace, now a weathered ruin, demonstrates the astute way in which the medieval bishops combined their personal lives and their spiritual responsibilities, with all the comforts of a worldly country gentleman. The palace lay in a fertile little valley and was surrounded by orchards, vegetable gardens and well stocked fish ponds. It also had its own windmill, dovecote and two watermills, while the nearby park supported a herd of about 60 deer, used for sport and to supply venison to the household. It reached its greatest splendour

Swanlake Bay.   © *Alan Shepherd Transparency Library.*

66

Freshwater East Bay from the air.   © *Alan Shepherd Transparency Library.*

under the powerful Bishop Gower (1327-47). In Elizabethan times it was the home of the great Devereux family, who later became the influential Earls of Essex. In 1821 it was purchased by Charles Delamotte Mathias who had inherited a fortune from family plantations in Jamaica. It now belongs to the National Trust and is carefully maintained. Mathias built the magnificent classical Georgian house, Lamphey Court, near to the palace. This is now a prestigious country hotel.

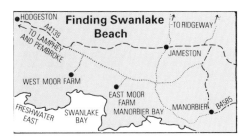

Freshwater East

Yet another fine expanse of sand with clear water and safe bathing. Quite a sheltered beach in the lee of Trewent Point, bounded by sand dunes. Usual beach facilities available.

Stackpole Quay and Barafundle Bay

Stackpole Quay is a quaint rocky little harbour, now only used by the odd lobster boat. Once a private quay for the Cawdor Estate, for the import of coal and the export of limestone from the adjacent disused quarry. In 1798 Lord Cawdor kept his yacht Speedwitch in this little harbour. Reached by lane from the Freshwater East-Stackpole road. Large car park

The Court, Lamphey.   © *A.S.T.L.*

67

Stackpole Quay and Cliffs to the East. © *Alan Shepherd Transparency Library.*

available. The name Stackpole is yet another example of the Norse influence in this area — Stak an isolate rock, Pollr — a small inlet.

Barafundle Bay can only be reached via the coastal path and the car park at Stackpole Quay is the best starting point. The beach is one of the finest in South Pembrokeshire, dune backed, especially fine sand, the sea is safe for bathing and crystal clear. Magnificent walks with spectacular cliff scenery in all directions*. No facilities.

The wall through which the path to the beach passes was originally built to keep the deer inside the Stackpole Estate. To ensure the preservation of the exceptional beauty of Barafundle, it was bought by the National Trust in 1976, along with a magnificent 8 miles of adjoining coastline.

* *See p. 144 for details of a walk from Broadhaven-Barafundle.*

Bosherston Village and Lily Pools

A pretty little village with a 13th century church, Village Inn (new) and quaint "Tea Rooms". Starting from the Car Park on your left as you approach the village, is one of the most beautiful walks in the National Park. This two mile stroll around the magnificent Lily Pools is highly recommended and is described in detail with further illustrations on p. 146.

Broadhaven Beach

Broadhaven Beach can be approached either via the Lily Ponds (footpath only) or by road from Bosherston Village (one and a quarter miles). Clifftop car park administered by National Trust (small charge). Unspoilt and rugged, but quite safe for swimming, with dunes, caves and cliffs to explore. Children will enjoy playing in the little river which invites paddlers as it meanders across the Northern side of the beach. Toilets, car park, steep path to beach. No other facilities. Undertandably, more people fall in love with Broadhaven each year.
(See also P. 144 for details of two superb clifftop walks from Broadhaven).

St. Goven's Chapel and Huntsman's Leap

(* **This area is part of the tank training range, and roads and paths may be closed for military manoeuvers at short notice. Notice of firing days can be obtained from local press, and from Bosherston Post Office. Distinctive red flags are also flown from prominent positions to indicate that the road is closed).**

Some one and a half miles past the village of Bosherston, the road ends at the top of the majestic grey windswept cliffs of St. Govan's Head (good car parking available). A narrow set

68

Barafundle Beach. © *Alan Shepherd Transparency Library.*

Bosherston Lily Pools. © *Alan Shepherd Transparency Library.*

of stone steps lead down from the clifftop to the tiny St. Govan's Chapel. History and legend intermingle in its background and it is difficult to determine its true origin. One of these legends links the chapel with Sir Gwain, one of the knights of the Round Table who is said to have turned hermit after the death of King Arthur. Current thinking dates it from around the 13th Century. There is also a tradition that no one can count the steps leading down the cliff to the chapel and re-count them on the way back up and arrive at the same total!

Rest for a while on the tangled mass of huge boulders, just below the chapel, and enjoy the spectacular views. Until comparatively recent times there was a fresh water well here, but this now appears to have been buried under fallen rocks.

By walking along the coastpath some 600 yards to the West of the chapel, you will discover the striking cleft in the cliffs known as "Huntsman's Leap" (the second ravine you come to). According to legend this gap was cleared by a huntsman at full gallop who, on looking back and examining his feat, promptly died of fright!

CAUTION The cliffs are high and near vertical, so do not let children wander off alone, and keep dogs on leads at all times.

St. Govan's Chapel.   © *A.S.T.L.*

Broadhaven Beach.   © *Alan Shepherd Transparency Library.*

Stack Rocks. © *Alan Shepherd Transparency Library.*

The short walk to Huntsman's Leap takes you directly into the army range and the wrecked target tanks which will doubtless fascinate the boys in the family, but they must only be viewed from the safety of the clearly marked path. Read the warning notices carefully, and on no account pick up any metallic objects for inspection.

Stack Rocks and The Green Bridge of Wales

Approached through the vast windswept expanse (over 6,000 acres), of the M.O.D. training Range. The lane winds past deserted farms, and Flimston Chapel, grey and sombre, its community long dispersed to

Huntsman's Leap. © *A.S.T.L.*

71

The Green Bridge of Wales.   © *Alan Shepherd Transparency Library.*

ST. CATHERINE'S GALLERY — Greetings, Christmas Cards and Prints of Pembrokeshire

If you are looking for images which reflect your love of the Pembrokeshire landscape be sure to ask for the St. Catherine's gallery collection of cards and prints. Designed by the author of this guide they utilise creative photography and the work of a number of accomplished watercolour artists.

Available from Art Galleries, Craft Shops, Bookshops and high quality Gift Shops throughout Pembrokeshire.

VIEWFINDER POSTCARDS

When choosing your viewcards to send to family and friends look for the distinctive Viewfinder range. Published by the author of this guide they combine high impact photography with original designs and portray the scenery and wildlife of Pembrokeshire at its exhilarating best.

Widely available at Bookshops, Newsagents, Gift Shops, etc.

make way for the tanks. There is a large car park and picnic area 150 yards from the cliff edge.

Before setting out to view the stacks, let your eyes roam over the surrounding landscape and note how level the land surface has now become. This section of the coast, in common with most of South Pembrokeshire, lay beneath the sea until some 17 million years ago. The sea was then some 200 feet higher, and the action of the waves planed off the higher parts of the land surface.

The two massive pinnacles of the Stacks — The Elegug Stacks (Elegug is the Welsh word for Guillemot), stand out proudly from a coastline which boasts some of the finest limestone cliffs in Britain. From these clifftops Guillemots, Razorbills, Kittiwakes, Gulls can be seen circling and soaring overhead and crowding the crags and ledges of the stacks.

About two hundred yards to the West of the stacks lies the dramatic natural limestone arch, known as the **"Green Bridge of Wales"**, springing from the turbulent surf, which washes over the wave cut platform below the cliffs.

A little to the East of the stacks lies the wild chasm of the **"Devil's Cauldron"**, entered

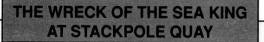

THE WRECK OF THE SEA KING
AT STACKPOLE QUAY

On October 16th, 1896, the Cardiff registered vessel, "Sea King," with a 16-man crew, left Barry docks in worsening weather conditions. Flying the Norwegian flag, and commanded by Captain Olsen, she headed down the Bristol Channel bound for Brazil with a cargo of 1,900 tons of coal from the Welsh valleys.

Though an experienced ocean voyager, Captain Olsen became alarmed at the rapidity with which the weather was deteriorating, and drove his ship hard in a bid to get clear of the rock bound channel coast and gain sea room. Off the Pembrokeshire coast the wind increased further to a full storm from the south east, when the ship was hit beam on by two enormous breaking waves which rolled her almost completely on to her side. Three men were washed overboard and all sails were either carried away or ripped to shreds. The steering gear was torn from its mounts and the bilge pump was rendered useless. Most serious of all, the weight of water crashing over the decks had loosened the main hatch covers and she was now taking dangerous amounts of water into the hold.

Realising that they would surely founder if they remained at sea, the captain knew that their only hope of survival was to run for the shore and beach the ship. In a great feat of seamanship the largely helpless vessel turned stern to the wind. She was now carried along by the weight of wind on her spars and rigging, and by the huge, breaking seas, which

rolled in a majestic surging procession towards the South Pembrokeshire coast.

Scarcely able to see through the breaking waves and flying spray, and without the ability to steer, the captain and crew must have watched mesmerised as the limestone cliffs near Stackpole Quay reared up out of the roar of the breaking surf ahead. From these cliffs a local shooting party watched with disbelief as the doomed vessel careered towards destruction. The impact of the crash was such that within ten minutes the ship had lost all form and was reduced to a heaving mass of timber, spars and rigging, through which men fought desperately for their lives. Only the captain and seven of the crew were rescued. Eight sailors perished, including one poor man whose body was hurled into a cleft in the rocks with such violence that it could not be recovered. The Pembrokeshire Herald reported.

"The man, who was wedged in a rock and could not be removed, presented a ghastly sight. The body now stands in an upright position, his head having been driven into his body by the falling of a tremendously heavy boulder on him. It is said to be impossible to remove the huge stone and so the remains of the poor fellow have to become the prey of carrion birds."

Tenby Lifeboat was in action during the same storm, and in all 18 men were rescued from vessels sheltering in Caldey Roads. The staging of the new lifeboathouse being built at Castle Hill was damaged.

Extracted from Welsh shipwrecks Vol. III by Tom Bennett.

Herring Gull.   *(Barrie Thomas)*

Puffin.   © A.S.T.L.

Bull's Laughter Bay.   © *A.S.T.L.*

The Devil's Cauldron, near Stack Rocks. © *A.S.T.L.*

by the sea through a wave battered arch. The near vertical sides of the blowhole go down for almost 150 feet, and the best views are obtained from the seaward side. This rugged little headland was once an Iron Age fort, and there are clear remains of early hut circles and defensive earthworks.

Those who venture a little further East along this rugged section of the coast footpath will be rewarded by lovely clifftop views of **Flimston Bay,** and after 700 yards of **Bull's Laughter Bay** (so named because the noise of the sea in the caves sometimes sounds like bulls laughing). The distance from the Green Bridge of Wales to Bull's Laughter Bay is almost exactly one mile. The clifftop is level and well drained, so even the non-walkers have no excuses!

Romulus and Remus

The children will enjoy stopping to look at these two tanks positioned dramatically at the entrance to the Army Camp at Merion.

Location: On leaving the road across the M.O.D. range from Stack Rocks, and rejoining the B4319, turn right for some 500 yards and the tanks are on your right. If you approach Stack Rocks from Bosherston instead of from Castlemartin you will drive past the camp entrance— on your left.

Castlemartin

A very small village; the church has a typical South Pembrokeshire battlemented tower. **The roundabout on the approach to the village is an 18th Century round stone cattle pound.** The village is surrounded to the south and east by the M.O.D. Artillery and Tank Training Range. In the summer months these are used by German Panzer Divisions. A viewing area has been created a mile or so to the East of the village (beside the Golden Plover Art Gallery), from which the frightening power and accuracy of the modern generation of tanks may be observed. In winter, these ranges are used to

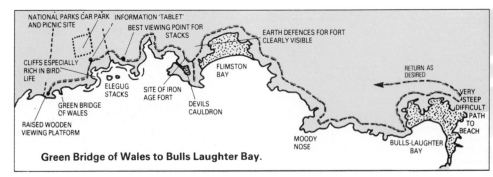

Green Bridge of Wales to Bulls Laughter Bay.

Freshwater West looking South towards Linney Head.   *© Alan Shepherd Transparency Library.*

graze large flocks of hardy Welsh sheep, brought down from the more extreme winter conditions on the Preseli Mountains. Just to the East of the viewing point is the small village of "Warren" with its prominent, but disused church, whose octagonal steeple is visible for miles in all directions, and is now maintained by the Admiralty, and used as a coastal navigation point.

Freshwater West

A majestic, unspoilt sweep of fine sand from which dunes roll inland. The southern, rather rocky corner of the beach is M.O.D. property and not open to the public. The beach is very popular with surfers as it faces due west and is subjected to the full force of the open Atlantic with long rolling surf breaking onto the beach for days on end during the winter. A dangerous beach for swimming, however, with strong currents and undertows. Lots of interesting rock pools for the children, and a freshwater stream runs down the beach. Those with an interest in collecting and polishing pebbles will also find plenty to interest them along the small pebble bank above the beach. Low spring tides can expose remains of a sunken forest and several ship wrecks. **An old seaweed drying hut** where seaweed was dried prior to the manufacture of **"Laver Bread"** still remains on

Romulus.   *© A.S.T.L.*

Not Welsh — but German!!   *© A.S.T.L.*

75

PEMBROKESHIRE SEALS

The seals found around the rocky cliffs and boulder strewn bays of Pembrokeshire are Atlantic Grey Seals. It is estimated that of 2,000-3,000 grey seals around the Welsh coast, most are located around the Pembrokeshire peninsula. Ramsey Island, off the tip of St. David's, supports the main breeding herds, especially the rugged west coast. Here around 200 pups are born annually. A similar number of pups are born to smaller groups of seals in tiny coves, isolated inlets, caves and remote rocky beaches scattered around the mainland coast and the other offshore islands.

Because man is a frequent "companion" in coastal waters off Pembrokeshire — pleasure boats, fishing trips, walkers on cliffs and beaches, the seals are not unduly frightened by the presence of humans. However, by nature they are timid and suspicious, and when in the water quickly submerge when startled. Because of their colouring and sleek shape they are often very difficult to spot in the turbulent waters around the rocks. They break surface extremely slowly, keep their heads well down and it is sometimes a little startling to find a pair of large dark eyes looking back at you from a patch of broken water. They are best observed basking in the sun on convenient rock ledges just above the waves, or hauled up resting on their favourite small beach, often at low tide. They tend to hunt at high water, and will often follow shoals of fish in very close to the shore.

Most of the seal pups in Pembrokeshire are born in late September or early October, and can weigh up to 30lb, at birth. They gain between 2-4lb a day for the three or four weeks when they suckle from their mothers. During this period the mother rarely feeds and can lose up to 100lb in weight. When the mother senses that the pup is strong enough to survive on its own, usually when its weight has built up to around 90lb she abandons it. The young pups then wander off to sea and cover long distances, coping with the worst of the winter gales whilst still only a few months old. Pups from Pembrokeshire have been traced to the West Coast of Ireland, the English Channel, West Coast of France and Northern Spain.

Seaweed Gatherer's Hut, Freshwater West. © A.S.T.L.

The Lagoon at West Angle Bay.   © A.S.T.L.

the headland. Car parking with spectacular views when rough. Toilets and ice cream available.

If the wind is on shore you may find it helpful to park in the small car park at the northern end of the beach and pick yourselves a sheltered hollow amongst the sand dunes. Just the place for building up that Pembrokeshire sun tan. During the late afternoon and early evening the children will enjoy a stroll over to the banks at the Angle end of the beach. Here a little patient observation will reveal that this sandy hillside with its covering of dwarf gorse and bramble scrub is an enormous rabbit warren.

Angle

A peaceful and rather remote little village with a long sea-faring tradition. **West Angle Bay** is a pretty sandy beach, and the adjacent Thorn Island with its fort, built as part of the defensive complex for Milford Haven, is now the Thorn Island Hotel. The views of Milford Haven are impressive and really large tankers can be seen entering and leaving the oil installations of this major port. The single long village street is an interesting collection of colour washed cottages, dominated by the colonnaded Globe Hotel and by the attractive village chuch. In the churchyard is a Fisherman's Chapel built above a crypt in

West Angle Bay from the air.   © *Alan Shepherd Transparency Library.*

West Angle Bay.   © *Alan Shepherd Transparency Library.*

THE DROVERS

Between the 9th and mid-19th centuries, Pembrokeshire was an important exporter of livestock. Herds of cattle, pigs and sheep were driven along the cross-country drover's road, thus avoiding the congested large towns and the tolls due on many of the main highways and turnpike roads. Farmers would deliver their herds of animals to specialist drovers at the collecting centres such as Haverfordwest, Crymmych and Whitland, from where they would set off on their long journey eastwards. Pigs were unpopular with the drovers as they could only travel about 6 miles a day, whereas cattle could often cover 20 miles per day. Many of the crossroads or resting places along the various routes had inns to house the drovers. These inns, often named "Drover's Arms" survive today. In South Pembrokeshire the herds of black cattle from the Castlemartin peninsula, and other livestock from the fertile fields of the great estates, finished their journey at Smithfield market where they were slaughtered to help feed the growing population of London.

CASTLEMARTIN POUND

IN 1480 THE PROPERTY OF THE LORD OF THE MANOR OF CASTLEMARTIN INCLUDED "A PINFOLD WITHIN THE COURT." THIS WAS PROBABLY THE PREDECESSOR OF THE PRESENT POUND WHICH DATED FROM 1780. IT WAS USED FOR IMPOUNDING STRAY CATTLE, WHICH WERE REDEEMED BY THE OWNERS ON PAYMENT OF A FINE.

THE POUND WAS RESTORED IN JULY, 1972 BY PEMBROKE RURAL DISTRICT COUNCIL

1447. On the opposite side of the road to the church, behind the houses is the only remaining ruined tower of Angle Castle, complete with its nearby dovecote and flanked by the original strip fields of the old feudal village.

There is a lifeboat station to visit and the fire in one of the village inns — The Point House — is reputed to have burned continuously for 300 years. Old seafaring men claim that the best anchorage in Angle Bay is so close to the Point House that the clock in the hall can be read through the front door, and they are probably quite correct. Angle Bay itself is shallow and muddy with several old wooden hulks. A popular refuge for ducks and waders.

Richard Strongbow set off from here in 1169 on his successful expedition to Ireland.

* Details of an interesting circular walk from West Angle Bay are given on page 147.

A second view of one of my favourite beaches — Barafundle (see p.68). © *Alan Shepherd Transparency Library.*

78

SOUTH PEMBROKESHIRE HOLIDAY COAST VISITOR AND INFORMATION CENTRE SERVICE

Situated at Tenby on the Croft overlooking North Beach, Tel. (0834) 2402, and at Kingsmoor Common, Kilgetty, Tel. (0834) 813672

Do you want to make the most of your holiday? Let friendly, trained staff help you to enjoy your stay in South Pembrokeshire by taking advantage of our various facilities. We can suggest days out to suit all ages and tastes and help with planning your entertainment by providing a continually updated "What's On" and "Activities" board.

We can book your Coach and Boat Trips, Walks and Talks Programme and Theatre tickets at no extra cost. We can advise you on suitable restaurants for that special occasion, an olde worlde pub or somewhere for just a quick snack. For those who have arrived without accommodation, we operate a bed booking service as well as a "book a bed ahead" service. We stock a comprehensive selection of free leaflets as well as a wide range of saleable publications.

Our opening times are:

TENBY TIC   Easter to end of October
                   10am to 5.30pm (7 days a week)
                   Extended opening hours in July
                   and August 10am to 9pm.

KILGETTY TIC   Easter to end of October
                   10am to 5.30pm.

Should you require a brochure please leave your name and address at the Tourist Information Centre to be entered onto our mailing list or contact us at the end of the year by writing to us at The Croft, Tenby, or telephone Tenby (0834) 2402 (24 hour ansaphone service).

LET US HELP YOU TO SEE THE BEST OF SOUTH PEMBROKESHIRE

Around the Pembrokeshire Coast

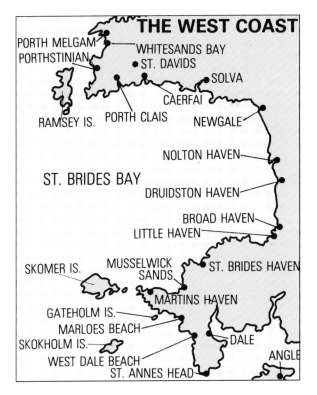

THE WEST COAST

PORTH MELGAM
PORTHSTINIAN
WHITESANDS BAY
● ST. DAVIDS
SOLVA
CAERFAI
RAMSEY IS. PORTH CLAIS   NEWGALE
NOLTON HAVEN
ST. BRIDES BAY
DRUIDSTON HAVEN
BROAD HAVEN
LITTLE HAVEN
SKOMER IS.   MUSSELWICK   ST. BRIDES HAVEN
SANDS
MARTINS HAVEN
GATEHOLM IS.
MARLOES BEACH
SKOKHOLM IS.
DALE
WEST DALE BEACH
ST. ANNES HEAD
ANGLE

Part Two
The West Coast

Dale to St. David's

Dale

Take the A4327 from Haverfordwest. Dale is a sheltered, quiet yachting village (the name is the Norse word for "Valley"), noted for its calm anchorage in the "Roads". The beach is mainly shingle but there is plenty of waterside activity in the summertime, and some magnificent beaches and scenery nearby. A good range of village facilities — pubs, shops, toilets, windsurfing school, etc. Car parking can present a problem.

It was at Dale that Henry VII landed in 1485 and proceeded to march through his native Wales, collecting supporters to win the great victory over Richard III at Bosworth, thus establishing the Tudor Dynasty.

Dale Fort above the village houses a Geographical Field Centre.

West Dale Beach

A beautiful little beach with good areas of rather coarse sand, bounded by bright red sandstone cliffs. The beach faces due West and must be treated with great respect. Dangerous and unpredictable currents and an uneven bottom make it hazardous for swimming. No vehicular access — use the pleasant footpath from Dale (half mile).

St. Anne's Head

A magnificent headland forming the Northern side of the entrance to Milford Haven. From the lighthouse, built on the original site of St. Anne's Chapel, there are

A Summer's Afternoon at Dale.

80

superb views in all directions, and you may be lucky and see one of the huge super tankers en route to Britain's premier oil port. As you stand at the lighthouse turn to face South West (towards the marker beacon offshore). Your nearest landfall would now be the coast of Florida some 3,000 miles away.

The lighthouse on St. Anne's Head has a history which can be traced to the middle ages when warning bonfires for shipping were lit on this dangerous headland. In fact, it is one of the oldest lights along the whole of the western coast of Britain. For many years it was the only light between the Scillies, off Cornwall, and the Isle of Man, far to the North.

The Lighthouse at St. Anne's Head. © A.S.T.L.

I hope the weather will be kind for your visit, but don't be deceived by this wide and apparently innocent harbour approach. Wind gusts of well over 100 m.p.h. have been recorded here and this whole area is littered with the wrecks of ships which misjudged the entrance. During a ferocious gale in November 1866, seven sailing vessels were all wrecked in one day on the cliffs of St. Anne's Head. It is thought that the first of these, running for the entrance at night, was overcome by mountainous seas and driven onto the rocks at Mill Bay. The other six ships then probably mistook the lights of the doomed ship for the market lights of Dale Roads and drove into this treacherous bay to their own destruction.

Littlehaven. © A.S.T.L.

Marloes Sands

Marloes Sands are to West Pembrokeshire what Freshwater West is to the South coast. Drive to the little hamlet of Marloes, park in the National Parks Car Park and then make your way by footpath to this glorious stretch of beach. A huge sandy expanse with lovely offshore views of the nature reserves of **Skomer** and **Skokholm Islands**. The Northern end of the beach has some interesting rock formations and is bounded by **Gateholm Island**. Gateholm is easily accessible at low tide and is the site of an early hutted settlement, probably an early monastery built around 600. Albion Sands lie on the Northern end of Gateholm and are so called after the paddle steamer Albion was wrecked here in 1837 — six months after making a record breaking trip from Dublin to Bristol in 21.5 hours. At low tide part of the wreck is still visible above the sand.

The beach at Marloes is quite safe for bathing, though some of the coves can be cut off by the rising tide. The cliffs are rather soft and unstable, and must not be climbed. No facilities.

At one time, leeches gathered by the villagers of Marloes from the nearby pond known as the Mere, were exported to Harley Street, where they were much sought after for "blood letting".

Martin's Haven

Attractive rocky cove with a shingle beach. This is the traditional harbour for the Marloes fishermen, and at one time over 20 boats operated from here. Now it is the departure point for the boats to Skomer, across the treacherous currents of Jack Sound. Park in the National Trust Car Park above the beach. The peninsula to the West of Martin's Haven is known as the **Deer Park**. It was once part of the Estate of Baron Kensington and the wall across it was designed to retain a herd of deer, which were, in fact, never introduced. At the end of a clear summer's day, some of the best sunsets in Pembrokeshire may be viewed from the vantage point of these cliffs.

Littlehaven

Pretty little cove nestling between high cliffs of brown shale. Plenty of sand at low water, but mainly pebbles when the tide is in. A popular boating centre for day sailing, with a convenient launching ramp. Car parking somewhat limited, but a pleasant sunny little village with good facilities. Difficult to imagine now, but once a coal exporting port for local collieries which have long closed. Small coasters were beached and loaded from horses and carts.

The walk past the Swan Inn out on to the **Point**, the headland to the South of the village, is

Lesser Black Backed Gull.

Razorbills.   (Barrie Thomas).

Adult Cormorant and Young.   (Mrs. A. Sutcliffe).

The Islands of the West Coast

Skomer

The largest of the Pembrokeshire islands — 2 miles long and 720 acres in area. It is a National Nature Reserve, owned by the Nature Conservancy Council and administered by the West Wales Trust for Nature Conservation. There is a resident warden during the summer months.

It is a lovely flat topped island exceptionally rich in sea birds. Vast colonies of guillemots and razorbills inhabit the ledges and deep fissures of the steep cliffs, and puffins are present in numbers. Kittiwakes, fulmars and choughs are also found, together with nocturnal Manx sheerwaters and stormy petrels. In September seals breed in some of the rocky bays. Reach the island by daily boat from Martin's Haven at 10.00, 11.00 and 12.00, return trips commence 3.15 pm. No landings on Mondays except on Bank Holidays. Also afternoon and National Park evening cruises. Tel: Dale Sailing Co., Neyland (0646) 601636 or any Information Centre.

Skokholm

The name is another legacy of the area's Viking past, HOLMEN is Norse for Island.

Skokholm lies 3 miles south of Skomer and has fine rugged cliffs of red sandstone. It is considerably smaller, with an area of 240 acres. The first Bird Observatory in Britain was established on Skokholm before World War II. There are large breeding colonies of sheerwaters, guillemots, stormy petrels, puffins, razorbills, gulls and oystercatchers. It also possesses a sizeable population of healthy rabbits which have escaped the ravages of myxomatosis. The National Park Authority organise excursions to Skokholm, weather permitting. Details from the Information Centres (p. 156), or contact the Dale Sailing Co. Tel: Neyland (0646) 601636.

Grassholm

Grassholm is a small island 10 miles out in the Atlantic, owned by the R.S.P.B.

It is the only gannetry in England and Wales with something over 20,000 pairs at present.

For landing and round trips contact Dale Sailing Co. Tel: Neyland (0646) 601636. Also National Park evening cruises. Tel: any Information Centre.

82

an enjoyable stroll with striking views
Northwards and Southwards along the cliffs of
St. Bride's Bay.

Puffin with Sand Eels

Broadhaven

Magnificent beach bounded by cliffs at
both ends. The **"Pembrokeshire Countryside
Unit"** is well worth a visit, with a good range of
educational materials. Bathing is usually safe,
although the rocky Northern headland area
should be avoided. Surfing possible under certain
conditions. Good beach and village facilities.
Large National Parks Car Park. Public launching
slipway. Youth hostel. Historically another of the
St. Bride's Bay beaches which was used for
exporting locally mined anthracite.

Nolton Haven

A pretty little hamlet set between high
bracken covered cliffs. Between 1850 and 1905 it
was quite an important coal exporting port for
anthracite from the nearby **Trefane Cliff
Colliery**. Coal was transported from the colliery
in pairs of 6-ton trolleys, pulled by traction
engines. Although the original quay, built in
1769, has gone, the rest of the old tramway, and
the **"Counting House"**, which administered the
harbour trade, can still be seen. Out under the
sea bed between here and Newgale it is estimated
that the coal reserves amount to over 230 million
tons.

Pleasant sandy beach well sheltered from
all winds, except those from the West. Do not
swim out towards the mouth of the cove, as this
can be very dangerous on an ebb tide.

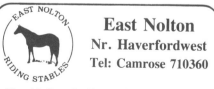

Broadhaven (North) from the air.   © *Alan Shepherd Transparency Library.*

Newgale

Vast sandy beach, the longest on St. Bride's Bay, backed by an impressive high ridge of shingle. The beach is easily accessible and car parking is good. Swimming is safe, and South West and Westerly winds often produce good surf. Boards may be hired. Beach and village facilities. The firm nature of the beach surface makes it an ideal winter venue for the exciting sport of Sand Yachting.

The small stream which runs into the sea at the Northern end of Newgale beach is the "Brandy Brook". **It marks the Northern extremity of "Little England beyond Wales".** Northwards, over the Landsker line, the other more rugged half of Pembrokeshire, the Welshry, with its much purer Celtic heritage, waits to welcome you.

Solva

(North on A478 Haverfordwest - St. David's road; 4 miles from Newgale).

A picturesque coastal village lying mainly in a narrow wooded valley, which leads to the harbour and on through cliffs clothed in bracken and wild flowers to the open sea. The village was for centuries a trading port and is quaint and well kept. Now a popular centre for yachtsmen. Solva has often been linked with smuggling and wrecking and some of the houses in the village have secret cupboards and shafts which might well have been used for hiding illegal goods. **Ogof** is the Welsh word for cave, and near Solva one of the local caves is called Ogof Tobacco!

At low tide there is some sand within the confines of the harbour, but the nearest sandy beach is the lovely **Gwadn Beach**, reached by footpath over the **Gribin Headland** to the East.

Nolton Haven.   © *A.S.T.L.*

This headland is also the site of two Iron Age settlements, and the climb to the ridge is well worth it for the impressive views in all directions.

Note the old **lime kilns** on the Eastern side of the harbour. Solva has a children's play area, shops, cafes, pubs and good accommodation. The **Nectarium** with its extensive collection of butterflies is not to be missed. Some car parking.

One mile North of Solva is Middle Mill, established in 1909, it produces tweeds and tapestries in traditional patterns.

One of the last of Pembrokeshire's coastal steamers was torpedoed by a German U-boat as she sailed from Solva in 1915.

St. David's
(via A487 from Solva)

St. David's ranks as a city only by virtue of the Cathedral built there in the 12th century, although at least three earlier buildings had been sacked and destroyed by Norse raiding parties between 800-1000 A.D. In all other respects it is an attractive, bustling village, sited at the natural cross roads of St. David's peninsula. The surrounding countryside is rather open and lacking in foliage and in winter is frequently lashed by fierce Atlantic gales. In the summer, however, the rugged splendour of the surrounding coastline, often ablaze

with gorse and wild flowers, lends the area a special atmosphere which has been jealously guarded against the more strident encroachment of tourism.

The Cathedral itself stands in a grassy, open valley to the West of the village, approached by the ancient thoroughfare of "The Peebles". Externally rather plain and subdued, the inside is surprisingly impressive with some superb roofwork of grey Irish oak. The oldest part of the present building is the nave which dates from the end of the 12th century, when the cathedral was rebuilt after destruction by the Vikings in 1078. Besides the shrine of St. David, who died here in 601 A.D., is also the tomb of Edmund Tudor, father of Henry VII. To the West of the Alun stream is the ruin of the Bishop's Palace, built in 1340 by Bishop Gower.

Bishop's Palace: Summer period 15th March - 15th October, 9.30-6.30 Mon.-Sun.
Winter period: 16th October - 14th March, 9.30-4.00 Mon.-Sat., 2.00-4.00 Sun.

THE ST. DAVID'S PENINSULA
PLACES OF INTEREST
Caerfai Bay
(see map)
Location: On entering St. David's from Solva,

The Old Farmhouse, Skomer Island.   © A.S.T.L.

The Farmhouse on Ramsey and Ramsey Sound.

THE LANDSKER LINE

Driving north from Newgale over the Brandy Brook you cross the **Landsker Line**, *and enter the more rugged* **Welshry**. *The following differences now quickly become apparent:*

a) Welsh is the dominant language almost everywhere. Note the place names.
b) The churches are usually smaller and less elaborate, with small bellcote towers. They are often located in isolated places where they were built to serve the scattered farming communities. In the south, the churches usually have a high battlemented tower, evidence of their defensive as well as religious role, during the period of Norman colonisation. They are often larger and more elaborate reflecting the greater agricultural prosperity of Little England.
c) Country settlements in South Pembrokeshire are often based on the Norman manorial system, of compact villages, with village greens around a larger church and with nearby strip fields. By and large the north has resisted this pattern and has retained its Welsh character with farms, smallholdings and cottages scattered randomly over the countryside.

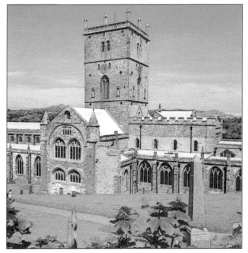

St. David's Cathedral.

St. Non's Well and Ruined Chapel
Location: Take the left turning off the one-way system in the village, following the signs for the Warpole Court Hotel. St. Non was the mother of St. David, the chapel is reputed to stand on the site of St. David's birth in 530 A.D. According to legend, the spring issued forth on the night of his birth. Beyond the well there is a small modern chapel set against the rugged backdrop of **St. Non's Bay.**

Porthclais
A small sheltered creek through which the River Alun flows to the sea.
Location: Bear left at the village one-way system, then straight on for one and a half miles.
According to Celtic folklore, the place where St. David was baptized.
Originally it was the small commercial harbour which served the religious community and the village in general, and until recently was still used by small coasters delivering coal. **The quay** and the **lime kilns** have been restored by the National Trust. Still used as a useful small harbour by local boatmen.

Porthstinian (St. Justinian's)
Location: (signposted from St. David's). Lying due West of St. David's, the beach is of shingle and stones but affords panoramic views over the

take the first turning on the left after passing the school on the right. Signposted.

A pleasant sand and shingle beach to the South West of St. David's, with some spectacular coloured rock formations and pools to explore. Clifftop car park with path to beach. Some of the stone for the Cathedral came from here.

The magnificent interior of St. David's Cathedral.

The Bishop's Palace, St. David's. © *A.S.T.L.*

Caerfai Bay, near St. David's. © *A.S.T.L.*

vicious tide rips of **Ramsey Sound** to **Ramsey Island** beyond. **St. David's lifeboat** is housed here and it is the departure point for boats to Ramsey Island. For many years it was used as a landing place by pilgrims coming to St. David's from all parts of the world.

    St. Justinian's Chapel was built by Bishop Vaughan of St. David's, on the site where St. Justinian was buried in about 500 A.D. Legend has it that St. Justinian was murdered on Ramsey, but managed to walk back to the mainland carrying his head!

Port Melgan. © *A.S.T.L.*

Ramsey Island

Ramsey Island is considered the most spectacular of the Welsh islands, with its magnificent cliffs and offshore islets, set in vicious tidal currents. It affords panoramic views of the mainland and even to Ireland on clear days.

The island is an important nesting ground for the delightful chough and also boasts breeding peregrine falcons. The sheer cliff faces support summer nesting colonies of kittiwakes, razorbills, guillemots and fulmars. On the beaches Ramsey has the largest breeding colony of Atlantic seals outside Scotland, and in the spring you may see more than a hundred on a single beach or, in the autumn, the cows suckling their pups. There is a large herd of magnificent wild red deer whose paths lead you through the rugged interior of the island.

Weather permitting, there is a regular ferry service from St. Justinians. Toilet facilities and light refreshments on the island.

For further information contact the Ramsey Island Shop, St. David's.
(Tel: 720648/720662).

Porthstinian. © *A.S.T.L.*

Grey Seal Pup. (Barrie Thomas).

Shrine to St. Non — Mother of St. David.

Whitesands Bay

Location: B4583 from St. David's. A magnificent sweep of fine sand with **St. David's Head** to the North and the 595 feet high **Carnllidi** dominating the beach just inland. Behind the beach is an undulating track of sandy ground, the burrows, now partly in use as a golf course. The beach faces due West into the turbulent Atlantic swell, and is one of the finest surfing beaches in Wales. Parts of the beach, however, can be dangerous for swimming and warning signs should be carefully noted. A popular beach during the height of the season, large car park, toilets, refreshments. For the really energetic, Carnllidi affords a stimulating climb, and the rocky summit commands views over most of the peninsula, Ramsey Island and the many treacherous outlying rocks.

The one mile walk northwards from Whitesands Bay to the lovely sandy cove of Porthmelgan is highly recommended.

Whitesands Bay with Carnllidi in the background.

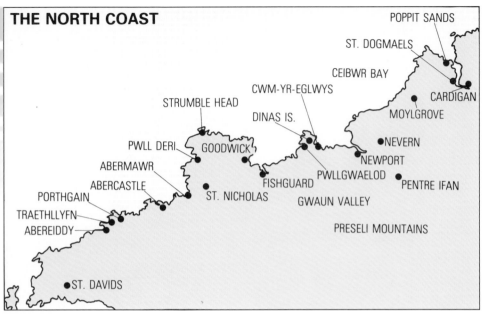

POPPIT SANDS
ST. DOGMAELS
CEIBWR BAY
CWM-YR-EGLWYS
STRUMBLE HEAD
DINAS IS.
CARDIGAN
MOYLGROVE
PWLL DERI
GOODWICK
●NEVERN
ABERMAWR
NEWPORT
ABERCASTLE
FISHGUARD
PWLLGWAELOD
PENTRE IFAN
PORTHGAIN
ST. NICHOLAS
GWAUN VALLEY
TRAETHLLYFN
ABEREIDDY
PRESELI MOUNTAINS
●ST. DAVIDS

Around the Pembrokeshire Coast

Part Three:
The North Coast
Abereiddy to Cardigan

Abereiddy
Quite a small bay with a rather sombre appearance, caused by the slate blue cliffs and dark sand. The row of ruined cottages originally belonged to the quarrymen who worked in the slate quarry on the headland. The quarry closed in 1904 and a narrow passage was later blasted into the foot of the quarry to provide a safe anchorage for small boats. Because of the blue effect of the slate this is known as the "**Blue Lagoon**". From the quarry workings, slate was sent to nearby **Porthgain** and the route of the old tramway can still be seen. The derelict cottages were overcome by waves during a storm in 1928. Plenty of car parking adjacent to the beach.

Porthgain
Leave Abereiddy and take the first left at **Llanrian**. A fascinating little creek dominated by the derelict workings of the old quarry machinery, engine shed, brickworks, lime kiln etc. Until 1931 some of the hardest granite known

was quarried here and the company — Porthgain Village Industries Ltd. — ran a fleet of six steam coasters of 350 tons each. Very small sandy beach beside the harbour. Plenty of car parking

Abereiddy. © *A.S.T.L.*

Porthgain Harbour. © *A.S.T.L.*

Strumble Head.   © *Alan Shepherd Transparency Library.*

space, pub and cafe. A visit to Porthgain is a must for those interested in industrial archaelogy.

Abercastle

From Porthgain return to **Llanrian**, turn left. Bear left at the next junction to **Trevine**. Keep left and head for **Abercastle**. A pretty little cove, well sheltered with a sandy beach — a popular spot for holidaymakers. Once quite a thriving little slate quarry port with a small shipbuilding yard for wooden vessels. Small car park, toilets and launching slip make this a popular venue for day sailing, diving and canoeing. The walk past the lime kiln and out along the western side of the harbour is highly recommended. Note the **old granary** on the opposite headland. Once you emerge onto the cliffs beyond the harbour mouth you have

Evening settles over Abercastle.

magnificent views Eastwards along a wild stretch of coast, towards the point at **Trwyn Llwynog** — but watch the cliff path, this stretch is not for those suffering from vertigo! Just across the fields (signposted) is the impressive burial chamber of **Carreg-Samson** with its huge capstone supported by three uprights.

Strumble Head

Dramatic rocky headland with its **lighthouse**, which was built in 1908 at a cost of £40,000. It is open to the public Monday-Saturday afternoon.

This very exposed spot is the nearest point to the Irish coast. The bay under the lighthouse is often used by seals. Overhead you will see the vapour trails of airliners come and go with a steady frequency because one of the homing beacons for Heathrow is nearby.

Goodwick

Continue Eastwards from Strumble Head and after 4¹₂ miles the road drops down the steep hill to Goodwick.

Sheltered by the enormous 2,000 feet long breakwater lies the commercial harbour for Fishguard at Goodwick! The building of the pier and the railway terminus took 11 years to complete. Originally designed as a **link with Ireland**, but also with an eye to attracting the **trans-Atlantic trade**. For some years the great Cunard liners **Mauretania** and **Lusitania** called here, but they had to anchor in the bay and

Demonstration by Lifeguards on Newport Beach.

unload by tender. Now a thriving ferry port for southern Ireland.

Fishguard

Curiously split up into the **Upper Town** with its shops, hotels, pubs and offices, and the **Lower Town** several hundred feet below at the mouth of the **Gwaun Valley**. Here is the old harbour with yacht moorings, quay and picturesque old fishermen's cottages (also Workshop Wales).

Plenty of activity around the old quay when the tide is in. For walkers, the headland opposite with footpath and strategically placed seats, provides an attractive stroll with lovely views. Access to this area is best achieved by

Lower Town and the Old Harbour, Fishguard.   © *Alan Shepherd Transparency Library*

War of Independence. It was also used as a location for filming Dylan Thomas's "Under Milk Wood" in 1971 when it became Llaregub.

In the Upper Town the Royal Oak Inn contains the tablet where Colonel Tate signed his famous surrender terms.

* Try reversing the letters in Llaregub and you have an insight into Dylan Thomas's impish humour!

Cwm Yr Eglwys and Dinas Island

Cwm Yr Eglwys is one of the most delightful little villages on the Northern coast, with some picturesque houses crowded, almost Mediterranean style, on the cliff edges. The cove has some car parking and good sand. The ruined church of **St. Brynach** at the waters edge was largely destroyed by a great storm on October 25th, 1859, when over 100 ships were wrecked off the Welsh coast.

Carningli Common

Approaching the outskirts of Newport from the direction of Fishguard take the sharp right turn signposted **Cwm Gwaun**. This delightful lane climbs high above Newport, with panoramic views of the surrounding coastline. Once you emerge onto the rocky, heather-clad moorland of **Carningli Common** you can park and picnic anywhere along the roadside. In August thousands of acres of heather are in bloom and the effect, when mingled with the vivid yellow gorse, is quite unforgettable.

Newport

A pleasant, interesting little town above the estuary of the river **Nyfer**. Plenty of attractive shops, inns and hotels. Some 18th and 19th century houses, sheltered by the Norman Castle.

leaving the car in the Lower Town and walking along the car and boat park in front of the **old granary** building, following the estuary as far as it goes. The path then climbs to the row of cottages where a sharp right turn soon connects you with the splendid **Marine Drive**.

Lower Town was bombarded by the famous pirate **Paul Jones**, during the American

Cwm-yr-Eglwys, near Newport (Pembs.)   © *Alan Shepherd Transparency Library.*

92

Pentre Ifan.

Sea bathing on **Newport Sands**, where is is possible to park on the beach. **Newport Parrog** is a more muddy beach, with some dangerous and unpredictable currents at certain states of the tide. The town also has an excellent nine hole golf course overlooking the sands and the estuary, as well as good boating and fishing facilities (bass and trout).

Pentre Ifan
Just over one mile to the east of Newport on the A487 turn right at Temple Bar (signposted) and make the detour to the great Neolithic burial chamber of **Pentre Ifan**.

Nevern
This quiet, attractive village lies in a beautiful wooded valley, with its church surrounded by massive yew trees. Legend has it that one of these trees, **the "bleeding yew"** will bleed until a Welshman is again Lord of the Castle on the hill (now little more than earthwork remains). Impressive **10th century Cross to St. Brynach** in the churchyard, and **Pilgrim's Cross** cut into the rockface near the road, about 100 yards beyond the village. First class salmon fishing in the river — **with appropriate permit!**

CELTIC CROSSES

Pembrokeshire has three surviving Celtic Crosses from the early Christian period. They are located at Carew, Penally and Nevern. The Carew Cross is one of the largest and most elaborately carved of all the Welsh crosses. It is inscribed to "Maredudd, Son of Edwin," a Welsh prince killed in battle in 1035. The cross is located in a rather dangerous position for viewing — right on the main road through Carew Village, near the entrance to the castle.

The attractive village church at Penally houses a 10th century wheel headed cross and the broken shafts of two other 9th and 10th century crosses.

The Nevern Cross stands 13ft high and is located in St. Brynach's churchyard in the shade of some fine ancient yew trees. It is also a wheel headed cross, intricately carved with Celtic style interlacements and key and fret designs.

Poppit Sands
A glorious stretch of firm sand extending along the Western bank of the Teifi estuary towards **Penrhyn Castle** and facing **Gwbert-on-Sea** on the opposite shore. Can be dangerous near the main channel of the Teifi, particularly when a spring ebb tide is running strongly.

Cenarth Falls. © A.S.T.L.

Cardigan.

Cilgerran Castle and Coracle Fisherman.

Lifeguard on duty during July and August, so pay attention to the warning signs and lifeguard flags. Delightful views towards Cemaes Head in the North West and Cardigan Island in the North East. Pleasant picnic site provided.

St. Dogmaels

St. Dogmaels straggles along the Western shore of the Teifi estuary and has a ruined **Benedictine Abbey**. Good fishing location (salmon and sea trout), and some lovely Inns to quench your thirst and swap tales about the great ones that got away!

* *St. Dogmaels Abbey — open any reasonable time.*

Cardigan

A very pleasant bustling little market town on the lowest bridging point on the Teifi. Enter the town over the fine 17th century bridge, now hard pressed to cope with volume of the 20th century traffic. The town has the remains of a Norman Castle and in 1136 was the scene of a shock defeat of the Norman-Flemish army, by the Welsh. Until the middle of the 19th century, Cardigan was the major port for this part of Cardigan Bay, but the development of the railway network led to the inevitable decline of coastal traffic. However, some riverside jetties and their old warehouses are still much in evidence. Good facilities and a variety of accommodation, plus some attractive new shopping areas. Ample car parking. A good touring base for the lovely old county of Cardigan and particularly suitable for fishermen seeking good river fishing (Teifi, Nevern and the Cych) and also for sea angling.

Cilgerran — Cenarth — Teifi Valley

Cilgerran

Two miles south of Cardigan — one mile east off the A478. This lovely old village with its impressive 13th century castle, set on a rocky outcrop high above the Teifi, is well worth exploring. In August the annual Coracle Regatta is held here.

Cenarth

Seven miles up the beautfil Teifi Valley from Cardigan on the main A487. Park in the car park adjacent to the old road bridge — next to the picturesque falls (small charge). Here the clear mountain waters of the Teifi are squeezed between narrow rocky banks and tumble over a series of stone outcrops and boulders on the way to the lower water meadows and the estuary at Cardigan. Fishing for salmon is the dominant preoccupation and traditional coracles are used in the pools below the bridge.

Inland Pembrokeshire

Part One:

The Towns and Villages of South Pembrokeshire

Cottage with Medieval Chimney, St. Florence.

St. Florence

A very pleasant and peaceful village, exceptionally well kept, having won the "Wales in Bloom" competition several times. In medieval times the village was connected to Tenby by the Ritec Estuary and St. Florence was a small port, even though it is now some three miles from the sea. Flemish influence can still be seen in the architecture. Very old village church. A wide range of accommodation and village pubs. The village is an excellent touring base for the south of the County. For walkers, a good network of footpaths radiates from the village with some delightful rural walks (use O.S. 1:25,000 Pathfinder Series No. SS09/19.

Carew

An interesting little village nestling beside a crossing point on the Carew River and dominated by a ruined but stately castle, dating from about 1300. There is a pleasant picnic area and car park opposite the castle from which viewing is recommended. At the entrance to the castle is a beautiful 11th Century Celtic Cross. Just down the river is the **French Tidal Mill**, which is the only tidal mill remaining intact in Wales. This has now been restored and is open

Carew Castle and French Tidal Mill.

Carew Castle

Carew Castle stands on a low limestone ridge above the peaceful Carew River and is surrounded on two sides by fine open meadows. The initial construction work on the site was started by Gerald Fitzwilliam of Windsor. Gerald was later given the primitive castle at Pembroke by Henry I in 1102, and it subsequently became his official stronghold, while Carew remained his private residence. The eldest son of this great warrior knight adopted the local surname de Carew and, thus, founded one of the greatest of the Anglo-Norman families of Wales. Much of the present day fortress was constructed by the celebrated Sir Nicholas de Carew, who built the immensely strong West Front, the chapel and the gatehouse. As the years passed and the kingdom became more secure, the strategic importance of the castle diminished and modifications were made which changed the nature of the building from a fortress to a fine Tudor home.

In 1480, Sir Edmund Carew handed over control of the castle to its most illustrious owner, Sir Rhys ap Thomas, and the lands passed out of the Carew family for the next 130 years. Sir Rhys was probably the most powerful nobleman in Wales at this time. He had joined the fledgling army of Henry Tudor when he landed at Dale and had been one of the major factors in Henry's victory over Richard III at Bosworth Field in 1485. Henry showed his gratitude to Sir Rhys by showering him with gifts and making him a Knight of the Garter. In 1507, to celebrate his admission to the order, Sir Rhys hosted the last great tournament to be held in Britain.

The Grand Tournament

Noblemen came from all over Wales to the great event and were housed within the castle. Outside, on the castle green, a huge tented encampment was set up to accommodate those of lesser rank. On St. George's Day, the whole company, led by Sir Rhys, rode over to nearby Lamphey Palace where mass was said by the Bishop of St David's. On their return to Carew the tournament began. Records reveal that over the castle entrance a picture was displayed depicting St. George and St. David embracing each other. The first event was a sumptuous feast, the entrance to which must have been spectacular:-

"In the open court, two hundred retainers in Sir Rhys's blue livery formed a line through which the guests passed into a lesser court, where were arranged figures clothed in armour bearing the escutcheons and coats of armour of Sir Rhys's ancestors."

The great hall was richly decorated with tapestries and the tables laid with the finest plate of the day. Numerous loyal toasts were drunk to the new king and queen and their young son. The whole feast was conducted against a background of music from the harp and interspersed with stirring tales from the bards. Several hours later, the assembled guests were so merry that jousting was postponed till the morrow!

Next day a blast from the horn summoned the knights to the jousting field, next to the castle. Sir Rhys appeared in an impressive suit of gilded armour on a fully decorated charger. Two pages on horseback, four footmen and one hundred retainers, wearing his blue livery, preceded him and a hundred followed him. This stately procession moved to the enclosed area of the tilting yard where tents had been set up for the combatants. After a thrilling morning of jousting, the afternoon was devoted to wrestling, throwing the bar, tossing the pike and other athletic sports. The following morning was given over to more tilting, while in the afternoon they hunted deer in the park, killing several bucks. The evening was spent feasting and watching a local band of retainers playing "theatricals." Next morning, the knights took their leave of Sir Rhys and made their way homewards. Perhaps the most remarkable feature of the whole glorious pageant was the fact that over 1,000 men had spent almost five days in close company, yet "Not one quarrel, unkind word or cross look had passed between them."

On Sir Rhys's death, the Carew estate passed to his grandson, Sir Rhys ap Gruffydd. He was later executed for treason on Tower Hill on 4th December, 1531, and his head displayed on London Bridge. Some years later, Sir John Perrot was granted the Lordship of Carew. Perrot's great contribution to the fabric of the castle was the construction of the imposing North Front with its huge mullioned windows, overlooking Carew River. This remains one of the finest examples of Elizabethan architecture in Wales. Although an Admiral of the Fleet and Lord Deputy of Ireland, he subsequently fell from favour with Elizabeth I. In 1591 he was arrested for high treason and died in the Tower of London, shortly before he was due to be executed.

In 1607, Sir John Carew became the owner, thus re-establishing the earlier links of his family with the castle. During the Civil War George Carew declared for the king. As the war ebbed and flowed, the fortress was surrendered to Parliament, regained for the king and finally lost to the Roundheads under the feared Col. Roland Laugharne. Laugharne bombarded the South Wall with heavy cannon and eventually breached it.

Between 1680-1690 the castle ceased to be the family home of the Carew family and has remained unoccupied since. Today, the castle is still owned by descendants of the Carew family, but it is administered and sympathetically tended by the Pembrokeshire Coast National Park Authority. An extensive programme of archaeological excavation is currently under way in the castle grounds and should unveil further valuable information on its rich heritage. A beautifully sited picnic area has been constructed opposite the castle.

The castle is open to the public throughout the summer. So why not give your imagination a day out as well. Stand on the castle meadow with the magnificent backdrop of tower, wall and buttress and let your mind drown out the raucous calls of the present tenants — the rooks and jackdaws. Now conjure up those stirring images of the Grand Tournament which took place on this same turf nearly 500 years ago. This riverside castle and its shadowy ghosts of the past will prove to be willing partners. Before long, the thunder of horses, the swirl of scarlet banners and the clash of metal will prove irresistible as your senses are assailed by sights and sounds from the most regal episode in its illustrious past.

Carew Battlements at Sunset.   © Alan Shepherd Transparency Library.

Blackpool Mill.

Lawrenny

Approaching this sleepy and remote village you will pass through the hamlet of **Cresswell Quay** with its quaint village inn and quiet river views. On reaching Lawrenny Village bear to the left. The lane now skirts the Cresswell River and there are superb views of wide tidal creeks and rich low lying pastures all the way to the

Lawrenny Yacht Station. Just beyond this, the car park affords magnificent views of the River Cleddau — the heart of the inland section of the National Park. Walk along the small shingle beach to the low point and more spectacular river views unfold. You are now looking out on to the **Daucleddau**. Upstream is Castle Reach with the white battlemented towers of **Benton Castle** rearing out of the thick oak woods which clothe the banks opposite. The castle was probably built by Bishop Beck of St. David's   (c. 1280). There is no public access.

Return to Lawrenny village. Bear left and

Lawrenny — The Yacht Station.   © *Alan Shepherd Transparency Library.*

Cresswell Quay. © *A.S.T.L.*

drive through the estate gates, past the church on your left. You will now reach a National Parks picnic site situated high on a bank with extensive views over the confluence of the **Carew and Cresswell Rivers**.

Landshipping and Blackpool Mill

Narrow, centuries old country lanes meander through peaceful farmland to **Landshipping**, a tiny hamlet with stone quay and fine river views across the entrance of the Western Cleddau. From Landshipping the road passes through soft and beautifully wooded countryside (**Minwear Woods**) to **Blackpool Mill**. This well preserved and picturesque water mill enjoys a lovely wooded location beside the Eastern Cleddau. Most of the machinery of the old mill is complete and there is a craft shop and tea room as part of this popular attraction. Nearby is Slebech Trail, a shady woodland walk through Forestry Commission property, overlooking the Eastern Cleddau River. (Leaflet "A Walk in Slebech Forest" is available from Information Centres).

Up until 1860-70 the Cleddau estuary villages of Carew, Cresswell Quay, Landshipping, Lawrenny and others on the Western side of the Haven were flourishing little trading centres, each with its own quay. Small sailing coasters crewed by 2 or 3 men arrived on the high tide and served local merchants and farmers by dealing in commodities such as farm produce, coal and culm, cloth, livestock, ale and wine. In some cases the original quays are still visible. Today, the extensive mudflats in these creeks are of special interest to ornithologists, as they are used by large numbers of wildfowl.

* Just one mile from Blackpool Mill is the popular "Oakwood" Adventure and Leisure Park — the largest activity park in West Wales and well worth a visit.

Llawhaden

Llawhaden is three miles north of the main A40 road at Canaston Bridge (signposted).

FLEMISH CHIMNEYS

Flemish Chimney at Carew. © *A.S.T.L.*

Throughout Pembrokeshire, from the Middle Ages onwards, the houses of many of the more affluent farmers and gentry would have featured huge fireplaces, topped by massive round chimneys. Later modernisation work often led to the original building being demolished, re-built and re-attached to the original fireplace and chimney. Subsequently, some of these buildings have decayed and either wholly or partially disappeared, leaving these impressive chimney structures largely intact and standing in isolation. Good examples are located in the villages of Carew and St. Florence.

Also of special interest are the enormous square chimneys which were built above massive fireplaces, often apparently out of all proportion to the needs of the building which they served. There are many examples all over South Pembrokeshire, e.g. Bosherston, Bangeston (near Stackpole), Penally, etc. Although all of these chimneys are referred to locally as "Flemish Chimneys," there is no satisfactory evidence to link them with the immigration of Flemish workers to the county in the 12th century.

The castle was built by the Normans as part of their defensive frontier against the troublesome Welsh in the north of the county, i.e. part of the **Landsker Line**. It also served to protect the possessions of the Bishop of St. David's — the episcopal Lord of the estates in this area.

Narberth

"Give me Narberth on a wet Saturday afternoon" was the reply made by a local squire when asked how he had enjoyed himself on a recent tour of Italy, reports H.M. Vaughan in his "South Wales Squires."

Today, Narberth is a busy little market town with its attractive Town Hall in the middle of the main street. When approached from the south there are some lovely views of the distant

View from The Rath, Milford.   © *A.S.T.L.*

The Eastern Cleddau, near Blackpool Mill.

Haverfordwest Castle.

Preseli mountains. Here the English speaking south of the county begins to meet the Welsh speaking north and the two languages blend quite naturally. A good touring centre with a variety of accommodation. Car parking is well catered for. Only fragments of the Edwardian castle now remain; open to the public some afternoons throughout the summer months. Check on the board at the castle entrance.

THE FOUR ESTUARY TOWNS

Milford

Founded in 1793 by Charles Greville. Among the earliest settlers were a group of Quaker whalers from Nantucket, New England, attracted by the commercial potential of the new market for sperm oil required for lighting the streets of London.

In 1888 Milford Docks were finally completed and by 1914 two thousand people were employed in the fishing industry and well over 200 smacks were based at the port. However, over-fishing of the western fishing grounds, together with other economic factors brought the industry into severe decline and now fewer than 45 men and a handful of vessels are still engaged in fishing. Milford is a sunny and spacious town and the well elevated Rath has impressive views along the length of the lower Haven.

Pembroke Dock

The growth of Pembroke Dock occurred after 1814 when the Admiralty selected the small coastal village of Paterchurch as the site of its new dockyard. The deep sheltered water of the Haven and its location away from the European mainland made it an excellent "safe" base for experimentation with the new technology of shipbuilding — steam propulsion, iron cladding, screw and paddle propellers. For the rest of the century Pembroke Dock was probably the most advanced shipbuilding yard in the world. In all, the dockyard built five royal yachts and a whole series of naval barques, brigantines, cruisers, gunboats and battleships. By 1880 the yard was employing over 3,000 men. In 1926 the town was socially and economically devastated when the government announced that the yard was to close.

Although on the fringe of the tourist area, Pembroke Dock is a pleasant place to visit, the wide streets, arranged on a grid-iron pattern, are a pleasure for motorists and pedestrians. There is a variety of shops and good car parking is always available — even in the height of the season.

Neyland

Originally known as "New Milford," Neyland was selected by Brunel as the terminus for the South Wales Railway. The rail link was completed in 1856 with the intention of

MILFORD HAVEN

The magnificent Milford Haven Waterway, one of the finest natural harbours in the world has drawn praise from many illustrious sources down through the ages.

William Shakespeare wrote, ".... how far it is to this same blessed Milford; and by the way, tell me how Wales was made so happy as t'inherit such a haven." (Cymbeline).,

Daniel Defoe, author of "Robinson Crusoe," and other famous works, described Milford Haven as one of the greatest and best inlets in Britain. " ... and some say a thousand sail of ships may ride in it and not the topmast of one be seen from the other."

In 1803, Lord Nelson stated that Milford Haven was the only seaport for commerce on the west coast of Britain, and that it rivalled Trincomalee in Ceylon as the finest harbour he had ever seen.

Brunel's "Great Eastern" at Milford.

"H.M.S. Hotspur" built at Pembroke Dock Dockyard, 1897.

attracting Trans-Atlantic passenger services and promoting the Irish Packet Services to Waterford and Cork. However, the Trans-Atlantic Services failed to materialise and the Irish Ferry Services transferred to Fishguard in 1906. The opening of the high level toll bridge across the Haven in 1975 led to the closure of the ferry service from Neyland to Pembroke Dock and the resulting by-passing of the town by all through-traffic. In recent years the new yacht marina and associated developments at Brunel Quay have breathed a new lease of life into the town. Waterfront now attractively restored. Good sitting out areas with fine views of the Haven and Cleddau Bridge. Convenient car parking.

Haverfordwest

Haverfordwest is the county town of the old county of Pembrokeshire. Its riverside wharfs reveal its past importance as a port — lying at the highest navigable point on the Western Cleddau. As a main bridging point over the river it also became a focus of all the more important routes and vied with Tenby and Pembroke for commercial supremacy. The older part of the town is dominated by the 12th century castle, built on a high craggy rock, overlooking this strategically important site. The name derives from Haver Fjord — corn inlet first used by a group of Viking pirates who settled in the region in the 8th century. Like so many other small West Wales ports, the arrival of the railway in 1853 quickly killed off the seatrade and it settled into its present-day role of administrative and distribution centre for the county. Haverfordwest is probably the best shopping centre in Pembrokeshire and has an attractive new indoor-market, which has been constructed partially out

over the river on piles. There is also a large indoor swimming pool and an excellent sports centre.

Part Two:

The Preseli Mountains, Llys-y-Fran and the Gwaun Valley

The Preseli Mountains

Take the A478 to Narberth and continue northwards to **Llandissilio** and **Crymych**. From Llandissilio the road climbs steadily, and glorious views of the southern slopes of the Preseli Hills unfold on both sides of this fine stretch of road. As you approach the outskirts of Crymych, turn left into the road signposted **Mynachlog-Ddu**. Follow this road along the foothills of the Preselis until you come to **Mynachlog-Ddu**, where you turn right at the junction and quite suddenly find yourself amidst magnificent mountain country. Here the rocky common with its simple stone memorial on your left to Preseli's greatest poet, **Waldo Williams** (1904-1971), is overshadowed from the north by the craggy heights of **Carn Menyn** on the right, and **Carn Sian** on your left. Make a short detour by turning left at the next road junction. After half mile you will reach the **Gors Fawr Stone Circle** on your right. This is the largest and most impressive of all the Preseli stone circles. Return to the orginal route which now weaves westwards over beautiful hill country. Here the pasture becomes rougher as it climbs, until it finally surrenders to the wet acid soil of the mountains. Rugged, windswept country where the hardy hill farmer tries to wrest a living from the reluctant land. Deserted crofts, now home to the moorland birds, reveal the difficulties involved. After 5 miles of really enjoyable driving the road meets the B4313. Turn left and arrive at **Maenclochog** — an interesting little hill village with a pleasant village green and church. From Maenclochog visit the traditional Welsh cottage home of **Penrhos Cottage** (see p. 121).

Location: From the centre of the village take the road signposted Llangolman and Efailwen. After some 400 yards turn right. Bear right at the next junction and Penrhos Cottage is on the right a little over a mile further on.

Return to Maenclochog. (Those wishing to visit **Llys-y-Fran** should detour here. Details of routes on page 110). Now follow the sign for **Cardigan**, skirting the little village of **Rosebush**. At the New Inn turn right on to the main B4328 Haverfordwest-Cardigan road, which climbs steeply towards the ridge line of the Preseli range. Note the huge scar of the deserted slate quarries behind Rosebush on your right and the extensive conifer plantations of the Forestry Commission. **Foel Cwmcerwyn**, the highest hill in the range (1760 feet) topped with its burial cairn lies to your right. As the road reaches its greatest altitude there is a convenient car park from which to survey the gaunt high moorland country of the Preselis which now extends for miles in all directions.

Most of the land across the Preseli tops is still common land, freely grazed by many thousands of sheep and smaller herds of hardy Welsh mountain ponies, belonging to the neighbouring farmers. In some places, as recently as 1920 peat and turf were cut for burning.

This is superb walking country — quiet and desolate, the home of buzzards, curlews, ravens, kestrels and skylarks. For those who enjoy solitude these hills offer perhaps the finest walking in the county. Although all seasons have their own particular attraction of form and colour in the Preselis, the hills are at their most alluring in late summer and early autumn, when the moors and heaths are covered in huge random drifts of yellow and purple from the dwarf gorse and heathers. However, care must be taken, because in places the ground is deceptively wet and boggy and the weather can change with remarkable speed. This sometimes brings the cloudbase down on to the hills and it is then all too easy to get lost. A good map, compass, warm, sensible clothing, walking boots and preferably a companion are, therefore, strongly recommended to those who wish to explore the hills in earnest.

The Preseli Mountains from Carningli Common.   © *Alan Shepherd Transparency Library.*

The Rebecca Riots

The sharp rise in the rural population, together with the harsh economic climate of the first half of the 19th century, led to growing social tensions in West Wales. Life was especially hard for the farmers and their labourers. Rents were high, agricultural prices were falling and the new Poor Law legislation led to much resentment. As the local turnpike roads were improved, the number of small turnpike trusts multiplied, and they collected their tolls more aggressively. To maximise income new gates were often introduced just as the lime carting season was about to begin. This simmering resentment eventually led to clandestine meetings being held, and elements within the rural communities decided to take the law into their own hands. The first attack took place on 13th May, 1839, at Efailwen, seven miles north of Narberth, when the "Daughters of Rebecca," disguised in women's clothes, complete with flannel petticoats, tore down the toll gate and burned the toll-keepers cottage, which had only been completed the previous week. One of the leaders of the rioters was Thomas Rees of Carnabwth, a large man and local pugilist. Because of his burly frame he experienced great difficulty in obtaining women's clothes to fit until Big Becca, a large lady from the neighbouring parish of Llangolman, came to the rescue. Thus, the protestors became known as the "Rebecca Rioters." The gate at Efailwen was re-erected, and seven special constables provided for its protection. However, on the night of 6th June, 1839, a mob of about 400 arrived and smashed down the gate and toll house, for the second time. Many of the attackers were again disguised. The rioters also drew inspiration from an obscure biblical text,

"And they blessed Rebekah and said to her may your descendants possess the gates of those who hate them."

Over the next few years these sporadic and violent riots spread over much of West Wales and many gates were reduced to rubble. At Pwll-Trap in Carmarthenshire the destruction of the gates was accompanied by a little pantomime which, afterwards, often prefaced the rioting. Approaching the gate "Rebecca" would enquire (in Welsh), "My children, this gate has no business to be here has it?." The reply would be a positive . "No! It has not." "She" would then ask what should be done with it and would receive the clear response that it should be destroyed. Professional troops, dragoons on horseback, local militiamen and special constables were drafted in to quell the rioting, but without success. Several "Rebeccas" were caught, tried and were deported to the colonies, but still David Williams the historian of the Rebecca Riots noted, "By day the countryside seemed quiet, but at night fantastically disguised horsemen careered along highways and through narrow lanes on their mysterious errands."

These riots, which have since been interwoven with colourful folklaw led to the authorities and landowners being given a powerful shock. In 1844 a parliamentary commission was appointed to examine the people's grievances. Legislation was subsequently introduced which removed many of the Turnpike problems. By 1845 peace had returned to West Wales, and the strangely clad night time marauders must have returned to their hard routine on the land feeling that their nocturnal adventures had been well worth the risk involved.

Llys-y-Fran

From **Maenclochog** make the worthwhile detour to Llys-y-Fran, an extensive country park and the largest fresh water lake in Pembrokeshire (clearly signposted from Maenclochog).

Llys-y-Fran has excellent facilities for boating and fishing with well-marked walks and several landscaped picnic sites. The view from the picnic site on the western side of the huge lake encompasses the entire lakeside area, set against the backdrop of the Preseli range. The complete walk around the lake covers a distance of some five and a half miles. The park represents a splendid alternative to the beaches on the busy days of high summer.

* Llys-y-Fran lake was formed by damming the **Swynfi River**. It now supplies much of Pembrokeshire with its drinking water and the entire park is meticulously maintained by Welsh Water.

After visiting Llys-y-Fran, two other nearby excursions are recommended. (1) **The Wallis Woollen Mill at Ambleston** (2) **Scolton Manor Museum and Country Park.**
Location: Retrace your route from Llys-y-Fran towards Maenclochog for nearly 2 miles and turn left into a narrow lane, signposted Tufton. On reaching the main Haverfordwest-Cardigan road (B4329), turn left and after approximately 1 mile Ambleston is signposted to your right. To find

Llys-y-Fran.   © *Alan Shepherd Transparency Library.*

Scolton Manor do not turn off the B4329 for Ambleston, but continue south towards Haverfordwest for another 5 miles. The entrance to Scolton Manor is clearly signposted, directly

The Gwaun Valley.

VIEWFINDER POSTCARDS

When choosing your viewcards to send to family and friends look for the distinctive Viewfinder range. Published by the author of this guide they combine high impact photography with original designs and portray the scenery and wildlife of Pembrokeshire at its exhilarating best.

Widely available at Bookshops, Newsagents, Gift Shops, etc.

off the B4329 to your right. Highly recommended — fine grounds and a spacious house with a wealth of exhibits, covering all aspects of Pembrokeshire's past.

Gwaun Valley

A mile or so after the B4329 road has crested the Preselis, near to the summit of Foel Cwmcerwyn, and begins its descent towards the north coast of the county, watch for an important left turn immediately after the cattle grid crosses the main road. This turning is signposted Cilgwyn, Trefdraeth, Nevern and Cwm Gwaun. This small lane has lovely views of the Preselis, but try to keep your eyes on the road! Bear left at both of the two forks in the road and you are then in the unspoilt, sheltered and very beautiful valley of the **River Gwaun**. This single track road with occasional passing places demands care and attention. If you have the time, park the car and explore on foot. There are two Forestry Commission picnic sites at **Sychbant** and lower down the valley at **Clyn**.

If the weather is too warm for exploring, take the lane at the top of the valley signposted **Cilgwyn** and **Newport**. This loops its way along the steep north slope of **Carningli Common** under the shadow of the **Iron Age Fort** perched high above and has superb views to the north coast. Stop and watch traditional candles being made at the Cilgwyn Candles Workshop, before enjoying a swim from the fine beach at **Newport**.

See the Best of Pembrokeshire by Car

One of the most enjoyable ways to explore a new area is from the comfort and convenience of your own car. The shared excitement and the real pleasure of discovering the wild splendour of the coast, or the sweeping heather clad landscapes of the Preseli Hills, or delving into the past in one of the magnificent riverside castles will provide you with holiday memories which will linger on into the grey fireside days of winter. **This section assumes that the interested visitor will make "Little England Beyond Wales" his holiday base, but will also want to explore the "Welshry" with its very different cultural background, its moors and mountains, its salmon streams and dominant Welsh language.**

The cultural and geographical divide between the two parts of the county provides you with a unique holiday environment — different from anything else that Wales has to offer.

Equipped with the detailed routes described in this section of your Guide, together with the fold-out Visitor's Road Map which covers the whole county, you will be able to visit all the main

Checking the route, Freshwater West.   © A.S.T.L.

tourist attractions which this lovely county has to offer.

All of the suggested places of interest referred to in these motoring tours have already been described in detail in the appropriate sections. Page references are therefore provided throughout to allow you to refer back to the relevant information.

Three Tours from Tenby

Tour One.

Saundersfoot to Laugharne Pages 36-43 and 52-58

1. **Tenby-Saundersfoot,** then via the coastal lanes skirting the beach at Coppet Hall and past the Hean Castle to Wiseman's Bridge.

2. **Wiseman's Bridge-Amroth,** via unclassified minor roads.

3. **Amroth-Pendine,** unclassified minor road.

4. **Pendine-Laugharne,** via the A4066

5. **Laugharne-St. Clears** via A4066.

6. **St. Clears-Kilgetty,** A477(T).

7. **Kilgetty-Tenby,** A478.

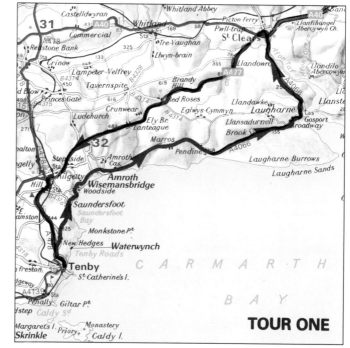

TOUR ONE

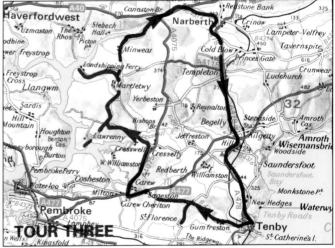

TOUR TWO

Tour Two. Penally to Freshwater East
Pages 61 to 67.

1. **Tenby-Penally**, A4139. Locate viewing point described above village at Strawberry Lane.
2. **Penally-Lydstep**, A4139. Stop for excellent views of Caldey, St. Margaret's and the cliffs at Giltar from the viewpoint 300 yards east of Lydstep village.
3. One mile after Lydstep turn left into **B4585**, signposted **Manorbier**.
   (a) Note the viewpoint and picnic spot described near to **Skrinkle Beach**.
   (b) Other magnificent roadside views of Manorbier beach and related parts of the coast are obtained as follows: Make your way to **Manorbier Castle** and take the lane down to the beach, continue past the National Park Car Park on the left, turn right over the little bridge and follow the narrow road as it climbs the hill on the western side of Manorbier beach. Parking with impressive views here.
4. Leave Manorbier on the **Pembroke-Jameston** road and rejoin **A4139**.
5. Turn left and drive 1 mile to Jameston, If you would like to visit Swanlake Bay turn to page 67.
6. **Jameston-Lamphey**, A4139 via **Hodgeston**, **Bishop's Palace** at Lamphey well worth a visit.
7. Turn left into the B4584 to **Freshwater East**.
8. Return to **Lamphey** and **A4139**. Drive over the railway bridge, continue for 130 yards, then turn sharp right into the road signposted **Tenby-Ridgeway**.

9. Return to Tenby via one of the highest roads in the South Pembrokeshire area — **The Ridgeway**. Spectacular views all the way, particulary at the eastern end above Penally.

Tour Three. Inland Villages — Carew Castle — Cleddau Waterway.
Pages 95 to 99.

1. Leave Tenby on the **B4318 Pembroke-Pembroke Dock Road**. This crosses the marshy bottom of the **Ritec Valley** at a spot where one of the last duels in Wales was fought in 1839. The 14th century **Gumfreston Church** on the left was once easily reached at high water by ships sailing up the Ritec Estuary. A well in the churchyard is said to have medicinal powers.
2. Lovely views across the Ritec Valley from **Gumfreston Top**. After another mile, pass the well-kept grounds of **Manor House Leisure Park** on your left.

3. Turn left into the minor road signposted **St. Florence**. Note the attractive church and **medieval chimneys**.
4. Rejoin the **B4318** and turn left towards Pembroke. Turn left at Sageston onto the A477 Carmarthen-Pembroke Dock road.
5. After approx 1 mile turn right into A4075 signposted **Carew and Haverfordwest**. Carew with its **13th Century Castle**, and **French Tidal Mill**, lies threequarters of a mile further on. Locate the **National Park Car Park** opposite the castle by turning first left after crossing the 17th century road bridge.
6. Rejoin the A4075 for approximately two miles, then turn left into a minor road to **Cresswell Quay and Lawrenny** — approximately 4 miles distant.
7. Follow your map carefully to reach **Landshipping** and **Blackpool Mill**. (This is a very rural area and roads are poorly signposted).
8. On leaving **Blackpool Mill** turn left and rejoin A4075. Turn left and some 300 yards further on at Canaston Bridge turn left in the direction of Haverfordwest only to turn right for **Llawhaden Castle** after some 200 yards (signposted). Return to the A40 at Canaston Bridge and then turn left for Carmarthen. After one and a half miles turn right at Robeston Wathen for **Narberth** (B4314).
9. Return to Tenby on the A478 via **Templeton** and **Begelly**. **Sentence Castle**, now only a mound, lies on the western side of Templeton village. Originally called **Gorsedd Arberth** and mentioned in the **Mabinogion**, the oldest of the recorded Welsh Tales, as one of the strongholds of Pwyll, Prince of Dyfed. Later, the Normans built a castle ring on the same site.

* Between Narberth and Begelly on the A478 you have the option to visit (i) the wildfowl centre at Herons Brook with its pitch and put golfing facilities (ii) Folly Farm — a large working Pembrokeshire farm. Both of these make excellent family visits. See pages 126 and 127.

Two Tours from Pembroke

Tour Four. Stackpole Quay — Barafundle Bay — Bosherston Lily Pools, Broadhaven Beach — St. Govan's Chapel — Huntsman's Leap.
Pages 67 to 70.

1. Take the B4319 south from Pembroke, following the signs for **Bosherston**. After some three miles look for **St. Petrox** church on the right. Just under a mile further on turn left into minor road marked **Stackpole**.
2. Park in the large car park behind the Quay and visit Barafundle Bay.
3. Re-trace route through Stackpole village to the junction with the B4319. Turn left and after half mile take left turn to Bosherston (the less severe turn of the two left turnings leading from the same junction).
4. In Bosherston park in the car park by the church and visit the Lily Pools.
5. Drive on through village and take left turn marked Broadhaven just past the St. Govan's Inn. Park in clifftop car park.
6. Return to Bosherston village, turn left and drive south for one and a half miles to St. Govan's Head. Visit St. Govan's Chapel, and Huntsman's Leap.
7. Return to Bosherston, then via the B4319 to Pembroke.

Tour Five. Angle — Stack Rocks and The Green Bridge of Wales.
Pages 71 to 78.

1. Take the B4320 west from Pembroke, via Monkton and Hundleton to Angle, approx. 10 miles.
2. Leave Angle via B4320, which is the only road in and out! and take the first right to the superb beach of Freshwater West, on the B4319.
3. Drive to Castlemartin and turn right at the "roundabout."
4. Follow B4319 along edge of the tank range for two miles then turn right into narrow lane signposted "Stack Rocks."
5. After two and a half miles on this lane which cuts across the bleak expanse of the tank

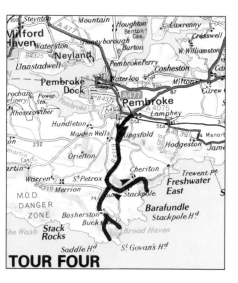

TOUR FOUR

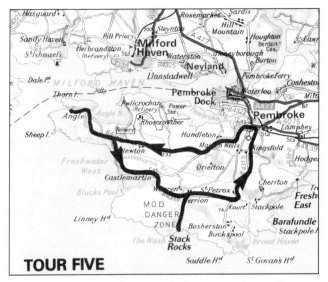

TOUR FIVE

the beach and **Dale Roads** before driving on to the lighthouse at **St. Anne's Head.** If you have the time **West Dale Beach** is well worth a visit.

2. Retrace your route out of Dale for a mile before turning left into the road for **Marloes.** Note the **clock tower,** given to the village by Baron Kensington.

3. Continue for two had a half miles to the car park above **Martin's Haven** and the **Deer Park.** Remember that Martins Haven is the embarkation point for Skomer Island.

4. Retrace your route to the B4327 and then, after less than a mile, turn left for **St. Bride's Haven.**

5. From St. Bride's cut "cross country," using minor roads, towards **Littlehaven.**

6. As you leave the village on the **Broadhaven** road watch out for the very sharp bend and steep incline.

7. At **Broadhaven** joint the B4341 and return to Haverfordwest via Portfield

range, park in the clifftop car park. See Stack Rocks, the Green Bridge of Wales and the other features described on pages 71-74.

6. Rejoin the B4319, turn right and after some 500 yards pass the two tanks, Romulus and Remus at the entrance to the army camp on your right. Follow the B4319 past St. Petrox to Pembroke.

Tour Six. The Dale Peninsula — Littlehaven and Broadhaven (North). Pages 80 to 84.

From Tenby make your way to Haverfordwest via Templeton (A478), Crosshands (A4115), Canaston Bridge (A4075), and A40.

1. Take the B4327 for approx. 12 miles to **Dale.** Park overlooking

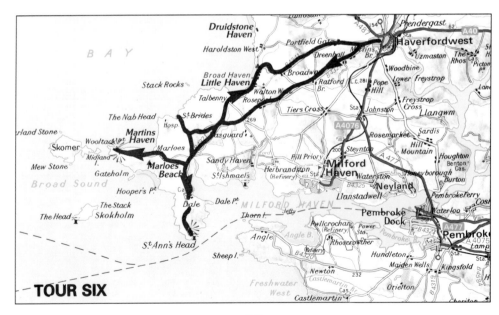

TOUR SIX

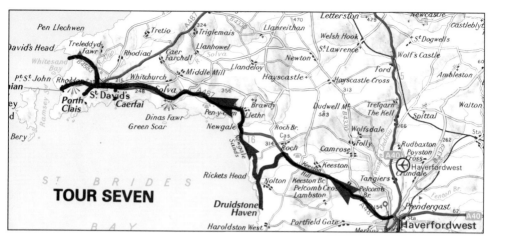

TOUR SEVEN

Tour Seven.
St. Bride's Bay and the St. David's Peninsula
Pages 83 to 88.

1. Leave Haverfordwest on the A487 road to **St. David's**.
2. At **Keeston** turn left and follow the signs to **Nolton Haven**.
3. From Nolton Haven make the short detour back along the narrow coastal lane to **Druidstone Haven** (see map).
4. Return to Nolton and follow the coastal road for several miles along the cliffs to **Newgale**.
5. Rejoin the A487 and head north for **Solva** — where the best car park is found at the head of the harbour.
6. Continue on the A487 to St. David's.
7. From St. David's visit (a) **Caerfai Bay**; (b) **St. Nons Well**; (c) **Porthclais**; (d) **Porthstinian** and **Whitesands Bay**. Full directions are given for locating these places of interest on pages 85-88. At Whitesands, if time permits, take the attractive cliff walk to **Porthmelgan**.
8. Return along the A487 to **Haverfordwest** and your home base.

Tour Eight.
The Rugged North Coast of Pembrokeshire
Pages 89 to 94.

1. From St. David's take the **B4583** road towards **Whitesands Bay**.
2. After only a few hundred yards bear to the right into a minor unclassified road (not signposted). This pleasant lane winds through fairly level coastal farmland for three and a half miles.

3. Watch for the left turning, signposted **Abereiddy**. Drop down to the beach and park in the car park.
4. Visit the **Blue Lagoon** and walk over the headland to **Traeth Llyfn** beach.
5. Leaving Abereiddy take the first left at **Llanrian** for **Porthgain**. Visit the pleasant little harbour which is steeped in recent industrial history.
6. From Porthgain return to Llanrian, turn left and then bear left at the next junction to reach **Trevine**. Keep left and head for **Abercastle**. Follow the coast path to visit the nearby burial chamber of **Carreg Samson**.
7. Locate the fine beach at Abermawr by taking the first on the left, then after 2 miles the next on the left. Limited car parking, so be prepared to park on the verge of the narrow lane to the beach. Visit the nearby **Tregwynt Woollen Mill**.
8. Stay on the winding coastal lane for a further 2 miles before turning left at a four-way crossroads to **Pwll Deri**. Use the small car park opposite the statue to local poet **Dewi Emrys**.
9. From Pwll Deri take the first turning on your left, then left again, then left yet again. When the road begins to descend towards the now clearly visible lighthouse at **Strumble Head**, take the first turning on your left, bear right before skirting the farmyard at Ty Daw to arrive at the car park above the lighthouse.
10. Drive to Goodwick and visit (a) the commercial harbour for cross-channel traffic to Ireland; (b) The Parrog.
11. Continue on the A40 to **Fishguard** and be sure to visit the quaint old Lower Town with its harbour at the mouth of the **River Gwaun**.
12. Return to the south of the county along the A40 to Haverfordwest via **Treffgarne Gorge**.

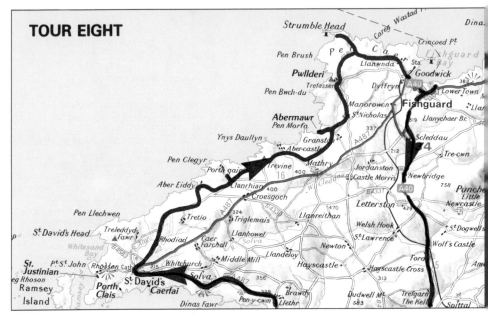

TOUR EIGHT

Tour Nine.

**The Preseli Mountains — Llys-y-Fran and Scolton Manor
Country Parks — Picton Castle Gardens.
Pages 101 to 104.**

1. From Narberth take the A478 road north
towards **Cardigan.**
2. After **Clynderwen** the road climbs steadily
towards the **Preseli Mountains** with fine views in
all directions.
3. Approaching Crymych take the left turning
signposted **Mynachlog Ddu.**
4. This road skirts the east of the Preseli Range
under the shadow of the **Iron Age Fort** at
Foeldrygarn.
5. At Mynachlog Ddu turn right on to
the open 'common.' Note the statue to
Preseli's greatest poet **Waldo Williams.**
6. Detour to visit the **Gors Fawr Stone
Circle** (left at the next junction, then
signposted on your right).
7. Continue along the
southern slopes of the
Preselis to **Maenclochog.**
Visit the traditional Welsh
cottage home of **Penrhos
Cottage** (see page 121).
8. Follow the signs for
Llys-y-Fran and visit this
huge lake and its magnificent
grounds.
9. From Llys-y-Fran make
your way to the **Wallis**

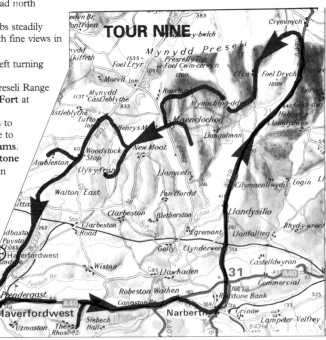

110

Woollen Mill and Scolton Manor Museum and Country Park (detailed directions given on p. 103).
10. Continue south on the B4329 to Haverfordwest (page 101).
11. Leave the county town on the A40 to Carmarthen. After approx. 4 miles turn into the minor road, signposted **Rhos**. Follow the signs for **Picton Castle** and park as directed.
12. Return to the A40 and make your way back to your holiday base via **Canaston Bridge**.

(page 101).

Tour Ten.
The Teifi Valley — The North East Coast — Carningli Common — Gwaun Valley
Pages 92-94.

1. From Narberth take the the a 478 north through the **Preseli Hills**.
2. Two miles past **Crymych** (after Blaenffos) run right into B4332, signposted **Cenarth**.
3. At **Cenarth** park in car park next to the bridge and visit the falls, salmon pools below the bridge and the Fishing Museum.
4. Take A484 south along the **Teifi Valley** to **Llechryd**. Turn left over bridge and follow signs for **Cilgerran**. Visit the castle high above the river.
5. Return via A478 road to **Cardigan** — the former administrative centre of the old county of Cardigan.
6. Re-cross stone bridge over **Teifi** and turn right into B4546 to **St. Dogmaels**. Visit the ruined Abbey.
7. Continue south along B4546 to **Poppit Sands** — large car park.
8. Follow coastal lane from Poppit to **Moylgrove**. Detour from village centre to **Ceibwr Bay** for spectacular cliff scenery.
9. Keep to coastal lane until you reach the village of Nevern. Visit the **Pilgrim's Cross, Celtic Cross** and **Bleeding Yew** in the churchyard.
10. Take the B4582 to **Temple Bar**, detour to Pentre Ifan (page 93).
11. Return to A487, turn left towards the town of **Newport** at mouth of **River Nyfer**.
12. From Newport make short detour to sheltered cove of **Cwm-yr-Eglwys** — 2 miles towards Fishguard on A487 — turn right before **Dinas**.
13. Return to the outskirts of Newport on A487 and turn sharp right for **Carningli Common** (signposted **Cwm Gwaun**).
14. Continue south across common, before dropping down steep escarpment into **Gwaun Valley**.
15. Turn sharp first left after hairpin bends and drive up to the lovely Gwaun Valley to rejoin B4329 Cardigan-Haverfordwest road at **Tafarn-y-Bwlch**.
16. Crest the Preselis and one and a half miles on, turn left at **New Inn** on to B4313, drive southwards to **Narberth** and then select your best route back to your holiday base.

TOUR TEN

What shall we do today?

When faced with the "problem" of choosing each day's activities, the holidaymaker in South Pembrokeshire finds himself in the happy position of being spoilt for choice.

This next section of the Guide is packed with ideas to help you to spend your days doing exactly what you like doing. Here you will find something for everyone — ideas for all ages and interests, for the energetic and the less so, and for days when the weather is less than kind. Many of these things to do will not put too much strain on your holiday budget, others are completely free. Pembrokeshire has it all — the choice is yours.

For easy reference, this section is organised as follows: Part One is for the energetic visitor, who likes to lace his holiday with excitement and activity. Here you will be able to find all those local sporting activities which reflect your own specialised interests.

Those who have a more languid approach to their holiday may want to skip this section and turn to **Part Two — Let's Have a Leisurely Day.**

Part One:

For the Energetic

Swimming Pools

If the weather is unkind and you cannot use the beaches, now is the time to take advantage of the local swimming pools. These are located as follows:

Tenby

Tenby and District Swimming Pool. A modern, 25 metre pool, plus children's training pool and flume. For seasonal opening times see current posters, local papers or phone Tenby 3575. The pool is located on the outskirts of the town at Marsh Road. It has a large car park (see Street Plan).

Park House Hotel, near Tenby also has a

Launching slipways in Pembrokeshire

NEWPORT
GOODWICK FISHGUARD

1 GELLISWICK
2 MILFORD HAVEN
3 HAZELBEACH

WHITESAND BAY
SOLVA
PORTH CLAIS
BROAD HAVEN
LITTLE HAVEN
BURTON LAWRENNY AMROTH
PENDINE
DALE 1-2-3 SAUNDERSFOOT
TENBY
NEYLAND
PEMBROKE DOCK

BEACH FLAGS — The warning flags used in the area are as follows:

Danger: Do not bathe	Lifeguards on Patrol: Swim between flags	Aqualung divers under water

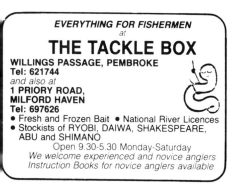

Karate Club on Holiday in Tenby.   © A.S.T.L.

lovely swimming pool as part of their sports complex, which is open to the general public. (Pool, Jacuzzi and solarium). Here you can also enjoy a poolside meal after your swim (p. 161).

Pembroke
Bush Sports Centre, between Pembroke and Pembroke Dock — part of Pembroke Comprehensive School Complex. Two pools. — Telephone: Pembroke 682462 for opening times.

Narberth
Pool situated in the old secondary school, Station Road. Opening times not finalised at time of going to press.

Haverfordwest
High Street. Tel: Haverfordwest 764354.

Sailing
The main sailing clubs in the south of the county are:
Tenby Sailing Club, The Harbour, Tenby. Tel: 2762.
Saundersfoot Sailing Club, The Harbour, Saundersfoot. Tel: 812492.
Neyland Yacht Club, The Promenade, Neyland. Tel: Neyland 600267.

Pembroke Haven Yacht Club, Hobbs Point, Pembroke Dock. Tel: 684403. Almost exclusively for sailing cruisers rather than dinghies.
Pembrokeshire Yacht Club, Gellyswick Bay, Milford Haven. Tel: Milford Haven 692799.
Dale Yacht Club. Tel: Dale 636362.
All of these Clubs extend a warm welcome to visitors and temporary membership is available.

Windsurfing
One of the most exciting of all watersports, windsurfing is becoming increasingly popular each season. Tenby and Saundersfoot bays offer excellent locations for novice and expert.

Weather Forecasts
BBC broadcast shipping forecasts on 1,500 metres long wave at: 00.33, 06.33, 13.55 and 17.55 every day.
Local sea areas - Lundy for South Pembrokeshire; **Irish Sea** for North.
Local forecasts - Swansea Sound 257 metres medium wave; Tel: (0792) 893751.
Cardiff Met. Office Tel: Rhoose 710343. Good advice can also be obtained from H.M. Coastguard. Tel: Dale 636218.

Surfing

The main surfing beaches in the south of the county are: Manorbier and Freshwater West. Freshwater West is not a beach for beginners, but its long rolling surf from the open Atlantic make it an ideal championship venue. In the north of the county, Newgale (where boards may be hired) and Whitesands, near St. David's are the best locations. The size and nature of the surf is of course totally dependent on wind and tide conditions at the time.

South Pembrokeshire Surf Club. Hon. Sec. Paul Ryder, 1 Axton Hill, Castlemartin. Tel: Castlemartin 661313.
North Pembrokeshire Surf Club, Chris Payne, 46 St. Bride's View, Roch. Tel: Camrose 710561.

Water Skiing

Burton, just north of the Cleddau Bridge,

is the main centre for organised water skiing in the county. However, most of the sheltered areas of the coast outside the bays can be used, but care must be taken to observe local speed-restrictions and bye-laws. (Check with Harbourmaster's Office at Tenby 2717, and Saundersfoot 812094). Saundersfoot Ski-School operates from the Harbour.

Diving

Dragon Diving Services, Castle Sands, Tenby.

Fishing

1. Sea Angling

The clear turbulent waters of the rugged Pembrokeshire coastline and the quieter waters of Milford Haven offer the sea-angler first class sport in unsurpassed surroundings. The county is renowned for bass fishing, but mullet, wrasse, pollack, coalfish, pout, gurnard, mackerel and dog fish are also caught. Among the flat fish population are flounder, plaice and "dabs." Some very large specimens of conger have been landed, often from the deep recesses of the Haven or around coastal rocks and wrecks. Larger, more exotic fish belonging to the shark family, e.g. tope, blue and porbeagle shark are also hooked from specialist boats, usually when they are in pursuit of the summer mackerel shoals. The most popular baits of lugworm, razor fish and mussels are, readily available from local beaches.

A wide range of fishing trips operate from Tenby and Saundersfoot harbours throughout the summer season, with options to provide good sport for beginner and expert. (Tackle and bait provided, if required).

FISHING INFORMATION

All game fishing throughout the region is private and permission must be gained from the landowner. A South West Wales River Board Licence is also required, usually obtained from a local tackle shop or from: National Rivers Authority, Llys Afon, Hawthorn Rise, Haverfordwest.
Tel: (0437) 760081.

Llys-y-Fran Reservoir's *trout fishing: 1st April-30th September. Licences and permits available at Office. Boat hire available. Tel: Maenclochog (0437) 532273.*

Rosebush Reservoir *brown trout fishing. Permit from the Water Bailiff, Blaenpant, near New Inn, Rosebush. Boat hire available.*

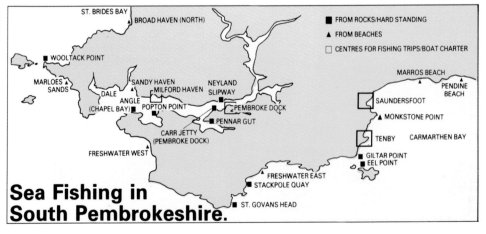

Sea Fishing in
South Pembrokeshire.

Fisherman at Sunset, Llys-y-Fran Reservoir, Mid-Pembrokeshire.

© A.S.T.L.

Sports and Activities — Surfing — Water Skiing — Diving — Fishing

2. Coarse Fishing

Bosherston Lily Pools are the best location in the county for coarse fishing. These lovely lakes are rented from the National Tust by the Pembrokeshire and District Angling Club — temporary membership available from local tackle shops and from the "Tea Rooms" in Bosherston village. Some fine specimens of pike, tench, roach and perch, together with large fresh water eels. (N.B. A Welsh Water Authority licence is needed as well as temporary membership to fish the lakes.)

3. Game Fishing

ivers in Pembrokeshire, ern Cleddau, provide good game fishing. A little further afield, the rivers Teifi and Taf offer top class fishing for salmon and sea trout. In the north of the county, the rivers Solva, Gwaun and Nevern attract considerable attention from those who enjoy fishing in quiet and beautiful locations. In the south, many of the small streams which flow into the sea, e.g. The Ritec in Tenby, contain brown trout. Llys-y-fran Reservoir in mid-Pembrokeshire is growing in popularity with anglers and it is well stocked with trout.

Other Activities

Golf

South Pembrokeshire Golf Club, Defensible Barracks, Pembroke Dock. 9 holes. Tel: 683817. Meals available.
Tenby Golf Club, The Burrows, Tenby. Tel:2787. 18 holes.
Haverfordwest Golf Club. Tel: Haverfordwest 763565. 18 holes.
Milford Golf Club, Hubberston, Milford Haven. 18 holes. Tel: Milford Haven 692368.
Newport (Pembs.) Golf Club. Tel: 820244. Pitch and Put facilities available at Herons Brook, Narberth. Tel (0834) 860723.

Squash

If the weather is unkind, why not enjoy an invigorating game of squash?
Courts available at:
Woodridge Leisure Centre, Wooden, Saundersfoot. Tel: 812259.
Bush Leisure Centre, Pembroke. Tel: 682461. *
Haverfordwest Leisure Centre, Prendergast, Haverfordwest. Tel: 765901.

Tennis

Tenby. Courts available at Greenhill School, Heywood Lane, Tenby * during school holidays.
Saundersfoot. Courts at Regency Hall. *
Pembroke. Bush Leisure Centre, Pembroke. *

(On A4139 between Pembroke and Pembroke Dock).
Pembroke Dock. Memorial Park. ★
Haverfordwest. Haverfordwest Leisure Centre (3 courts). Public Court, The Parade, St. Thomas Green. ★

Bowls
Tenby Bowling Club, Southcliff Street, Tenby. *
Saundersfoot Bowling Club, Regency Hall. *
Pembroke Dock, Memorial Park. *
Haverfordwest, The Parade. *
Temporary members are welcome at all clubs.

Putting
Tenby, The Bowling Club, Southcliffe Street.★
Saundersfoot, Regency Hall. ★
Pembroke Dock, Memorial Park. ★

Badminton
Bush Leisure Centre, Pembroke.★
Haverfordwest Sports Centre (opposite Sir Thomas Picton School).★

Bicycle Hire
J. Codd, Cross Inn Garage, Broadmoor, Kilgetty. Tel: Saundersfoot 813266.

Horse Riding and Pony Trekking

Riding Centres
Island Farm, Devonshire Drive, Saundersfoot. Hourly hacks and treks. Tel: Saundersfoot 813263.
Norchard Farm Riding School Manorbier, Nr. Tenby. (Licensed and Approved). Horses and ponies to suit all ages and abilities. Novice riders always welcome. Daily rides, treks and lessons amidst some of the loveliest countryside in South Pembrokeshire. Tel: Manorbier 871242.

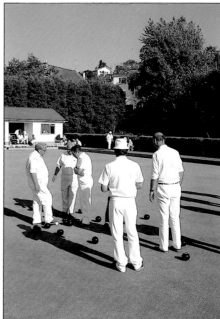

Evening Bowls Match, Regency Hall, Saundersfoot.

★ See appropriate Street Plan.

Sports and Activities — Bowls — Putting — Badminton — Shooting — Riding

117

Part Two:
Let's Have a Leisurely Day

Family Picnic on Manorbier Beach.

Pembrokeshire is a "browser's" paradise, and its general pace of life will ideally suit those with a more relaxed attitude towards their holiday. Use the dozens of ideas on these pages to help you to plan ahead.

Coastal and River Cruises

On a hot summer's day, what could be more enjoyable than to board one of the large, well equipped boats plying from Tenby Harbour, or from Hobb's Point, Pembroke Dock, for an extended cruise? Relax in comfort, listen to the interesting commentaries of the skippers. Choose from the rugged splendour of Caldey and St. Margaret's Islands with their bird and seal colonies, or the quiet wooded beauty of the upper reaches of Milford Haven, or, as a complete contrast, the awe-inspiring size of the super tankers and the vast multi-million pound oil installations of the lower Haven. Whatever your choice, you will not be disappointed.

Coastal and Island Cruises of Tenby

Invite you aboard one of our two 100-seater passenger vessels for a coastal cruise along some of the most spectacular National Park Coastline in Britain. Options available include:

- The Islands Cruise around the Monastery Island of Caldey and the Bird and Seal Sanctuary of St. Margarets.
- Two Coastal Cruises. 1. – along the wooded cliffs of the North Bay, passing the sunken forest at Amroth. 2. – southwards past the fretted limestone cliffs of Giltar to Lydstep Caverns and the Smugglers' Caves.
- The Extended Cruise past the Norman Castle at Manorbier to St. Govan's, Stack Rocks and the renowned Green Bridge of Wales.
- Barbeque Cruise (Wed at 7.30 during July/Aug only) evening cruise followed by a barbeque on the patio of The Imperial Hotel – overlooking Caldey Island.

Each boat is fully equipped with a large covered saloon, fully licensed Bar, Children's Sweet Shop and Toilet. Relax and let your experienced skipper's commentary help you to enjoy to the full the exhilarating coastline and its rich wildlife

Further details from: Our Harbour Office or
'Sheerwater', St. Julian's Terrace, Tenby.   **Telephone: Tenby 3179**

Things to do — Coastal and Island Sea Cruises

Local Museums

Milford Haven Museum. Compact, but attractive museum, featuring all aspects of the evolution of the town. Contains a wealth of material on the fishing industry, and has a distinctly maritime flavour. Run exclusively by volunteers. Situated in Mansfield Street.

Narberth Museum. The Old Court House, Market Street. Tel: Narberth 681266.

Art Galleries

The Graham Sutherland Gallery, Picton Castle, The Rhos, Haverfordwest. Houses largest collection of Graham Sutherland works on exhibition anywhere in the world.

Tenby Museum and Art Gallery, Castle Hill, Tenby.

The Castle Museum and Art Gallery, Haverfordwest. Tel: 763708.

Artists' Studios/Galleries

Fron Studio and Gallery, Llanycefn, Clynderwen. Tel: Maenclochog (0437) 532313. Gallery shows the work of Denis Curry D.F.A. (Slade), professional painter and sculptor. Situated in a traditional Pembrokeshire Hill Farm, the Gallery is open at all reasonable times, although a telephone call beforehand is advisable.
Golden Plover Art Gallery, Warren,

Things to do — Museums and Art Galleries — River Cruises — Day Trips to Ireland

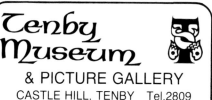

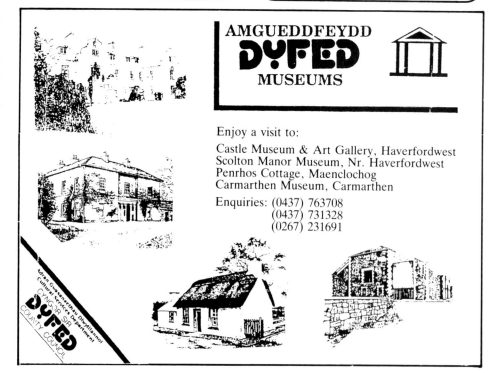

Craft Shops, Cob Lane, Tenby.   © *A.S.T.L.*

Penrhos Cottage near Maenclochog.   © *A.S.T.L.*

Castlemartin. Bim and Arthur Giardelli. View by appointment. Tel: Castlemartin 661201.
Harbour Gallery, St. Julian Street, Tenby. Featuring the work of John Cahill R.C.A. Open all reasonable hours throughout the summer season.
The Coach House, The New Quay, Haverfordwest. Tel: 67694.
Workshop Gallery, Workshop Wales, Lower Town, Fishguard. Tel: 872261. High quality Gallery exhibiting work of well known and up and coming artists.

Island Photographic Gallery, 36 Nun Street, St. David's. Tel: 720433. The work of Jacki Sime, Wildlife Photographer.

Mills to Visit

Carew Mill. This mill dates from the reign of Queen Elizabeth I, when it was let to John Bartlett for the sum of £10 per annum. It is the only tidal mill now remaining intact in Wales. The present three storey building dates from the 19th century and it was used for grinding corn to

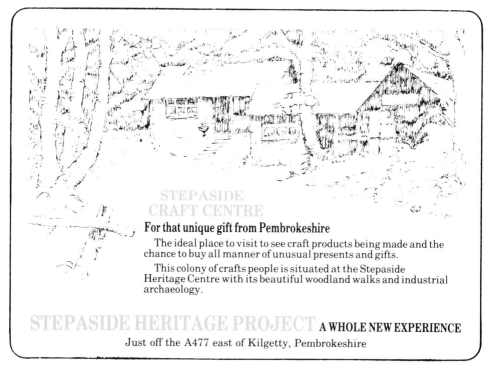

STEPASIDE
CRAFT CENTRE

For that unique gift from Pembrokeshire

The ideal place to visit to see craft products being made and the chance to buy all manner of unusual presents and gifts.

This colony of crafts people is situated at the Stepaside Heritage Centre with its beautiful woodland walks and industrial archaeology.

STEPASIDE HERITAGE PROJECT **A WHOLE NEW EXPERIENCE**

Just off the A477 east of Kilgetty, Pembrokeshire

𝔓embroke 𝕮astle

Pembroke Castle is the oldest in West Wales and for over 300 years was the seat of the Earls of Pembroke. It was founded by the Mongomerys in 1093 and work began on the splendid masonry a century later with the circular Great Tower or Keep. Dominating the Castle, the Tower stands fully 75ft high and is the finest of its type in Britain. Home to such great personalities as Earl William Marshal, regent to Henry III, and the early Tudors, Pembroke Castle can boast the birth of a king within its walls – Henry VII or "Harri" Tudor. During the Civil War the Castle was held firstly for Parliament and then for the King. Cromwell arrived in person to lay siege to the Castle which led to its final surrender.

OPENING HOURS
The Castle is open to the public daily at the following times:
1st April-30th September (including Sundays) 9.30am-6.00pm
March and October (including Sundays) 10.00am-5.00pm
November to February (closed Sundays) 10.00am-4.00pm
The Castle is closed to the public on Christmas Eve, Christmas Day, Boxing Day and New Year's Day.

ENTRANCE FEES
Adults £1.50 Children (under 16) and OAPs 80p
Family Tickets (2 Adults plus 2 children) £4.00.
Student Parties pre-booked 70p
Parties of 20 or more pre-booked £1.30 and 70p.
Primary School Parties pre-booked 40p
Season tickets by arrangment
Children under 5 and physically handicapped (in wheelchairs) FREE.

FURTHER INFORMATION
Address: Pembroke Castle Trust, Pembroke SA71 4LA.
Telephone: Office (0646) 681510. Ticket Office: (0646) 684585

Manorbier

A CASTLE WITH A DIFFERENCE

Life-size figures on display recreate the history of this fine Castle dating from the 12th Century.

The Castle, which encloses attractive gardens is situated overlooking picturesque Manorbier Beach, five miles from Tenby and Pembroke.

Open:
Easter for 1 Week and from 18th May to 30th September.

Visiting Hours:
10.30 a.m. to 5.30 p.m.
Souvenir Shop during Opening Hours
Rail & bus transport is available.
Details from local information centres.

---

produce flour until the First World War. The rising tide is allowed to fill the mill pond upstream of the mill where it was stored. As the tide falls, the head of the water is then released through a sluice where it turns the main mill wheel, which in turn powers the auxiliary machinery inside the mill. The mill has recently been renovated and is open to the public from April to September (inclusive), 10 am-6pm weekdays; 2 pm-6 pm Sundays. (Entrance fee charged).

Wallis Woollen Mill, Ambleston, Nr. Haverfordwest. Interesting old mill in quiet valley, 15 minutes from Llys-y-Fran Dam. Pure wool floor rugs and fine worsteds.

Tregwynt Mill. This working woollen mill is situated near St. Nicholas in the north of the county.

Local Craftsmen and Craft Workshops
Potters. Pottery is one of the earliest crafts and in South Pembrokeshire its tradition is still kept alive and healthy by a number of skilled local craftsmen operating in small studio workshops. Each has developed his own personal artistic style and a variety of practical or decorative specialities. They all welcome visitors and will often undertake commissions to your own requirements.

       Alan Hemmings Associates Ltd.

"Studio in the Church," **Login.** Handweaving in mohair. Beautiful things from Wales. Mon.-Fri. 10-5 pm. East of Efailwen on A478.

Workshop Wales. Lower Town, Fishguard. A craft centre where a number of self-employed craftsmen produce a range of beautiful craft goods — furniture, clocks, chess sets, lamps, clothing, cards, posters, toys, etc. Signposted from "Lower Town Harbour." Open 10 am-6 pm every day during summer. If you undertake the Preselis - Fishguard tour, allow time for this interesting visit.

Antique Shops

For those with a special interest in antiques, Pembrokeshire offers exciting possibilites. The contents of many of the remote farms and large country houses come on to the market quite regularly, and highly sought after pieces of all kinds, especially furniture, find their way into many of the excellent local antique shops. So don't stand with your noses pressed to the window! — Walk in, you'll find plenty to interest you. The owners are often a mine of information on their particular speciality, and are always delighted to share their enthusiasm with an interested customer.

Auction Sales

Narberth. Monthly auction sales are held

Attractive paperweights created by local craftsmen at Avondale Glass, Kilgetty.

Furniture made by local craftsmen at Solva.

124

Blackpool Mill, Caves & Cafe

(Just off the A40 at Canaston Bridge)

A delightful riverside corn mill with operating turbine and wheel. See the superbly restored machinery, model steam engine, display of riverside wildlife, fishing coracles and caverns showing prehistoric hunting scenes.

- ● **Craft shop and Cafe for homemade lunches and teas**
- ● **Peaceful walks in the Pembrokeshire National Park**
- ● **Open: Easter to 30th October. 11 a.m. – 6.00 p.m.**

**Blackpool Mill, Canaston Bridge, Narbeth, Dyfed
Telephone: Llawhaden (09914) 233**

A GREAT DAY OUT
in 80 acres of beautiful
Pembrokeshire countryside.

Nutty Jake's Music Hall Show,
Goldmine Ride & Goldrush Town
Treetops Rollercoaster
Daring Waterfall & Bobsleigh Rides ☆ Pirate Ship ☆ Huge Undercover Playland
Go Karts ☆ Assault Courses ☆ Boating Lake ☆ Cinema 180°
Skyleap ☆ Mini Golf ☆ Orienteering ☆ Nature Trails
RESTAURANT ☆ FAST FOOD ☆ SHOPS

OPEN DAILY at 10am Easter – end Sept   Restricted opening in October
ALL INCLUSIVE ENTRY PRICE
Oakwood Park, Canaston Bridge, Narberth. Tel: (0834) 891 376

Places to Visit — Activity and Leisure Park — Riverside Corn Mill

HERON'S BROOK

COUNTRY PARK AND WATERFOWL CENTRE
NARBERTH

An ideal setting for those who want an enjoyable day out in the country.

★ Large variety of birds and waterfowl
★ Picturesque picnic areas & woodland walks
★ Play area and pets corner
★ Supervised pony rides
★ Croquet area and putting green

18 HOLE PITCH & PUTT

CAFE – SNACKS – SOUVENIRS
OPEN 10am – 6.00pm EASTER
Then from 1st May-30th Sept.
Tel: Narberth (0834) 860723
Location – just outside Narberth on the A478 Tenby Road

Pembroke Dock. Every Friday in Melville Street **Carmarthen Market.** Large covered market with excellent cross section of stalls including antiques, crafts, bric-a-brac, fresh produce, etc. Wed. and Sat. 7 am-5 pm (some stalls open every day).

Local Markets and Livestock Marts

Tenby Market in the Market Hall, High Street, Butchers, Greengrocery, Fish, Haberdashery, "Rock" and Confectionery, Pet Supplies, Welsh Clothes and Fabric.

Haverfordwest Market. Good cross section of units, housed in attractive new building built partly out over the River Cleddau.

New Hedges Open Air Market. Every Thursday (in field off the roundabout near the Crestville Motel).

Carmarthen Livestock Mart. One of the largest in Wales, and probably in Britain. Large number of animals bought and sold weekly. Monday and Wednesday. Mornings are the most interesting. Come and see the West Wales farming community at work. ("Wellies" may be a good idea for the children).

Country Marts. Much smaller local marts at Haverfordwest (Tuesday), Cardigan (Saturday), St. Clears (Tuesday and Friday), 10.30-3.30.

Silent World Aquarium

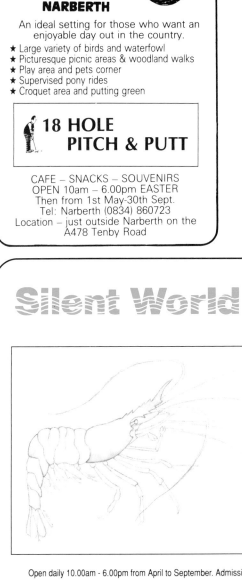

and WILDLIFE ART GALLERY

WHAT OUR VISITORS SAY
— "peaceful and beautiful"
— "thoroughly enjoyable and exciting — excellent use of a lovely building"
— "Very informative for both young and old"
— "It just goes to show you don't have to be big to be beautiful"

Find us on the map square 2D, near Slippery Back.

Open daily 10.00am - 6.00pm from April to September. Admission: Adults £1.50, Senior Citizens and children 4-16 75p.

Silent World Aquarium, Slippery Back, Narberth Road, Tenby. Telephone (0834) 4498

There's more to this farming than I thought! Trainee Dairymaid at Folly Farm.

Places to Visit — Working Pembrokeshire Farm

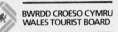
Carmarthen

Carmarthen is the most lively shopping centre in West Wales, and is easily reached by road and rail from all over Pembrokeshire. It sits astride an ancient bridging point over the wide river Towy — where fishermen still fish for salmon and sewin from quaint coracles. The fertile Towy Valley, stretching inland from Carmarthen, is the premier dairying region of Wales, and on mart days Carmarthen is invaded by the farming community, in numbers. Its once notorious traffic jams are now only a memory, thanks to the by-pass and new river bridge.

Why not combine a day out to Carmarthen, perhaps on mart day to really sample the local atmosphere with a visit to one or more of the other major attractions presented on the next few pages.

Pendine and the Dylan Thomas Boathouse at Laugharne

Those travelling from South Pembrokeshire turn right off the A477 at Red Roses. If approaching from North Pembrokeshire on the A40, turn into the A4066 at St. Clears.

Holiday Reading

The Pembroke Book Shop, 73 Main Street, Pembroke (Tel: 685144). Maps, guides, natural history, children's books and a wide range of holiday reading.

Gwili Railway, near Carmarthen.

The Wind Energy Demonstration Centre at Carmarthen Bay
Located at Burry Port, south of Carmarthen on the A484. This route passes the formidable Kidwelly Castle, the nearby Industrial Museum and skirts the extensive Pembrey Country Park with its fine beach.

The Gwili Valley Railway
Situated in an attractive wooded valley at Bronwydd Arms, a few miles north of Carmarthen on the A484 Newcastle Emlyn road. One for boys of all ages!

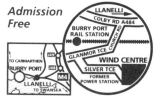

A Day out in Carmarthenshire

DYLAN THOMAS'
BOATHOUSE MUSEUM, LAUGHARNE

Over the past 10 years, the Boathouse has been sensitively developed into one of Wales' foremost heritage attractions, welcoming visitors from all over the world.

A visit to the Boathouse, whether with family, friends or as part of a school/party group really does offer an unusual afternoon out.

With its superb setting overlooking the Tâf Estuary, the attraction houses an Art Gallery; Bookshop; memorabilia; original writings and furniture; audio and visual presentations and a charming period tea room. Open from Good Friday and all year for school/group tours.

Tel: 0994-427420 (the Boathouse) or Carmarthen 234567 (Tourism Section, Carmarthen District Council).

Just a car ride away!

A Day out in Carmarthenshire

Family Walks to Explore the Best of South Pembrokeshire

Walkers at Lydstep enjoy the view. © *A.S.T.L.*

Pembrokeshire as a whole and particularly the 225 square miles of the National Park area, offers those who enjoy walking unrivalled opportunities. There is something for everyone. The feast of the 167 mile coast footpath for the dedicated enthusiast, well equipped with O.S. maps and lightweight backpack, and for the less ambitious, a gentle stroll across the beach at Freshwater West, with a cooling paddle on the way back to the deckchair, newspaper and a cup of tea from the thermos.

The walks that follow have been carefully selected to bring you into direct contact, as only walking can, with many facets of the unsurpassed landscape of South Pembrokeshire. Through these walks — many of which are circular — you will appreciate the full grandeur of the coast, the significance of major historical sites, and the surprising richness of recent industrial history. Those completing all these walks will have experienced the unique atmosphere of "Little England Beyond Wales," and probably succumbed to its heady appeal. So lace up your boots, reach for your anorak and enjoy yourself. If you have a pair of

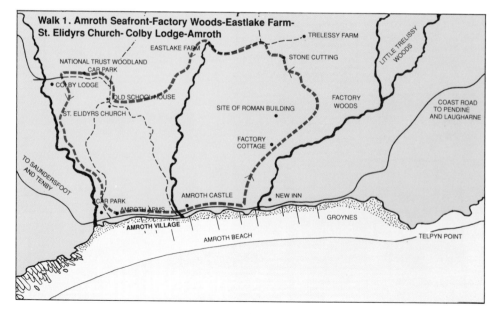

Walk 1. Amroth Seafront-Factory Woods-Eastlake Farm-
St. Elidyrs Church- Colby Lodge-Amroth

TRELESSY FARM

LITTLE TRELISSY WOODS

EASTLAKE FARM

STONE CUTTING

NATIONAL TRUST WOODLAND
CAR PARK

COLBY LODGE

OLD SCHOOL HOUSE

FACTORY
WOODS

COAST ROAD
TO PENDINE
AND LAUGHARNE

ST. ELIDYRS CHURCH

SITE OF ROMAN BUILDING

FACTORY
COTTAGE

TO SAUNDERSFOOT
AND TENBY

CAR PARK

AMROTH CASTLE

NEW INN

AMROTH ARMS

GROYNES

AMROTH VILLAGE

AMROTH BEACH

TELPYN POINT

132

binoculars remember to bring them, and of course your camera.
* *The two O. S. maps for Pembrokeshire are Sheet 158 (Tenby) and Sheet 157 (St. David's and Haverfordwest).*

1. Amroth Seafront — Factory Woods — Eastlake Farm — St. Elidyr's Church — Colby Lodge — Amroth.
A circular walk of approximately 3.5 miles, featuring superb woodland sections rich in bird life.

Use your map to reach Amroth village, on the coast some six miles east of Tenby. Continue along the seafront through the village and park, as convenient, between Amroth Castle and the New Inn, at the extreme eastern end of this huge beach. Locate the public toilets and the track marked "Bridleway" leading off the seafront between the two white houses. Just past the cottages fork right on to the wide gravelled trackway which climbs gently through the trees, away from the coast.

The woods are typical of many in South Pembrokeshire, occupying the steep unusable portion of a valley bottom and composed of stunted oak, beech, elderberry, sycamore and holly, all with a generous under-foliage of assorted ferns and bracken. On the hill-top above is the site of a Roman settlement. A few hundred yards past Factory Cottage the track curves to the left and the gradient steepens as we climb the valley side and skirt Factory Wood — the large expanse of woodland below and to the right. Local enquiries reveal that this wood was probably so called because at one time there was a small "factory" on the site producing wooden clogs for local use. The track is quite steep and bounded by a rocky culvert, down which a small stream gurgles on its way to the sea. Levelling out a little, the path passes a small stone cutting before swinging left and finally emerging onto open farmland at the top of the valley.

This is an elevated, breezy area of small bright green fields and neat, well-trimmed hedges. The sea is now screened from view by low, wooded hill-tops and Trelessey Farm, away to your right, casts a watchful eye over its domain. At the crossroads turn left over the heavy metal cattle grid into the gravel driveway of Eastlake Farm. Watch the electric fence on your left as you drop down gently towards the attractive farmhouse and the next steep-sided, wooded valley. Below the farmhouse locate the gap in the fence on your left and pass to the left of the modern milking parlour and cattle yard. Climb the wooden style and bear away down a wide grassy path towards the fine stand of mature conifers which occupy the valley bottom.

Approaching the stream the path narrows and passes banks of brambles, bracken and scrub, which are usually alive with many species of small, woodland birds. A large concrete slab carries the path over the stream. It is quiet and restful here. On hot days the tall conifers cast welcome shade and the birds will probably be your only companions. The busy sea-front at Amroth, crowded with traffic, now seems many miles away.

After regaining your breath, set off up the opposite slope, following the right fork in the path. At the top of this bracken-covered incline,

PEMBROKESHIRE COAST NATIONAL PARK

Information

A number of lectures and guided or accompanied walks are available in Pembrokeshire, from early April to late September. The guides are experts in ornithology, natural history, archaeology, geology and other related subjects.

In South Pembrokeshire the walks are usually well attended and cover areas like Mynachlog-Ddu (Preselys), Llys-y-Fran, Llawhaden, Slebech Forest, Cleddau Estuary, Stepaside, Tenby, Waterwynch, Penally and The Ridgeway, Freshwater West and West Angle. The lectures are usually held at the Information Centre, Kilgetty. For details contact the Information Centres at Tenby, Pembroke, Kilgetty and Saundersfoot.

The Country Code

Enjoy the countryside — respect its life and work.

*Guard against all risk of fire.
*Fasten all gates.
*Keep dogs under control.
*Use gates and stiles to cross fences, hedges and walls.
*Leave livestock, crops and machinery alone.
*Take your litter home.
*Help to keep all water clean.
*Protect wildlife, plants and trees.
*Take special care on country roads.
*Make no unnecessary noise.

Spring at Colby Lodge Gardens, Amroth
    © Alan Shepherd Transparency Library.

Trust. Visit the impressive walled garden with its stylish, Victorian summer house and, if time permits, the Woodland Walk. The latter exposes the wealth of fine specimen trees and shrubs which make the garden one of the finest in South Pembrokeshire. Opening times: 31st March to 3rd November. Admission charge made.

Our path heads due south along the heavily wooded flank of the eastern side of the valley. A few hundred yards from Colby Lodge the magnificent setting of the house, which was designed by John Nash, becomes fully apparent. Here the valley opens out and forms a natural bowl, where wooded slopes merge into rich grassy meadows. In the valley bottom a stream makes its unhurried way towards Amroth and the sea. In early spring the stream banks are awash with colour as thousands of daffodils nod their heads to welcome the lengthening days of the new season. This section of the walk under the high bank of beech, oak, holly, rhododendron, etc., is especially rich in birds and you will see and hear chaffinches, thrushes, blackbirds, blue-tits, sparrows, robins and magpies.

After some distance, locate the white-washed farmhouse and outbuildings, hard against the woods on the far side of the valley, reached by its bridge of railway sleepers over the stream. Some 300 yards on bear right at the fork in the path. The valley is now much narrower and stream and path stay in close proximity. Rounding a gentle left hand bend, the houses of Amroth re-appear ahead. Re-join the village lane and walk down through an interesting collection of well maintained properties with trim gardens, all vying for a sea view over the bay. Pause at the Amroth Arms and imagine the same scene only 60 years ago. The open sea-front opposite and to the right was occupied by a whole row of substantial terraced houses — fronts to the road, back to the sea. These and the land occupied by Burrows Hall, a large block of garages opposite Temple Bar Inn, together with Cliff Cottage, where the public conveniences now stand, at the foot of the hill out of the village, have long been pounded to rubble and washed away by the winter storms. Even today with the new sea wall in position, the sea-front properties are occasionally battered by huge seas, whipped up by southerly gales, which block the road with mounds of pebbles carried over the sea wall. Turn left up the slope past the Post Office, and opposite the final cottage, "Mole End", take the concrete walk above the "new" sea wall.

This roughly follows the line of the old coast road to Amroth Castle, which also succumbed to the merciless attention of the sea in the 1930's requiring the cutting of a new section of the road further up the cliff. This final seafront section makes a pleasant way back to your car.

where the pine needles crunch under your feet, leave this peaceful wooded valley, through the pair of ancient, domestic-style gates, often secured with red baler string! Emerging into a rough, overgrown field, follow the hedge to the opposite left-hand corner. The square, battlemented tower of St. Elidyr's church is now visible through the trees and bushes ahead. If cattle have been using the final section of the path the ground may be heavily cut up and muddy, so pick your way carefully. Negotiate the two wooden styles, pass the ruined cottage and reach the country lane below the church. Turn right.

St. Elidyr's is an attractive church, sturdy and compact, with its cluster of tightly packed weathered gravestones and dark green yew trees. The little church seems dignified and aloof on its hill top setting, somehow strangely detached from the busy seaside village it serves, on the coast below.

Fork right at the church leaving the "Old School" on your left. After 150 yards turn left into the side road signposted "Colby Lodge Gardens". Leave the National Trust Car Park on your right and descend steeply through magnificent mature beeches and banks of rhododendrons to Colby Lodge, nestling at the head of the beautiful valley below. Just below the high stone wall of the walled garden turn sharp left into the outbuildings of this attractive property, now administered by the National

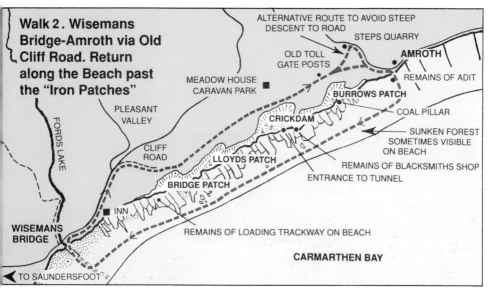

Walk 2. Wisemans Bridge-Amroth via Old Cliff Road. Return along the Beach past the "Iron Patches"

ALTERNATIVE ROUTE TO AVOID STEEP DESCENT TO ROAD

STEPS QUARRY

OLD TOLL GATE POSTS

AMROTH

REMAINS OF ADIT

MEADOW HOUSE CARAVAN PARK

BURROWS PATCH

COAL PILLAR

PLEASANT VALLEY

CRICKDAM

SUNKEN FOREST SOMETIMES VISIBLE ON BEACH

FORDS LAKE

CLIFF ROAD

LLOYDS PATCH

REMAINS OF BLACKSMITHS SHOP ENTRANCE TO TUNNEL

BRIDGE PATCH

INN

WISEMANS BRIDGE

REMAINS OF LOADING TRACKWAY ON BEACH

CARMARTHEN BAY

TO SAUNDERSFOOT

2. Wiseman's Bridge — Amroth via the Old Cliff Road. Return to Wiseman's Bridge, tide permitting along the beach, past the old iron "Patches". Circular Walk: 2.5 miles.

Use your map, if necessary, to locate Wiseman's Bridge, on the coast just a mile or so east of Saundersfoot. Parking is usually available on the top of the pebble bank beside the road, but it can be a squeeze in high season. When you arrive at Wiseman's Bridge check the position and direction of the tide. This may demand that you reverse the direction of the walk described and head for Amroth along the beach first.

Climb the main coastal road leading from the western side of the beach, past the popular Wiseman's Bridge Inn. Treat this road with caution, it can be busy and there are no grass verges for refuge. After 400 yards bear right into Cliff Road, marked with a cul-de-sac symbol. It should also carry a wooden sign for Coast Path, but this was broken the last time I used this route. Climb steeply up Duncow Hill, once the site of a coal yard used as a collection point for the local mines. Leave the tarmac road at the turning circle and take to the cliff path — signposted. Much of the coast path between Wiseman's Bridge and Amroth follows the route of the old "Cliff Road". Notice the width between the overgrown side hedges which would easily allow passage for a horse and cart. This exposed, but direct, route was used for many years by carriers driving coal from the Saundersfoot collieries to Amroth, Pendine, Laugharne and beyond.

Some 300 yards after leaving the turning

circle locate the boundary stone in the left hand hedge, marked L.M. These initials stand for Lord Milford, former owner of a huge estate in this area.

Boundary Stone marked with initials of Lord Milford.

Amroth through the Pine Trees above the village.

135

Three of the old iron Patches on the cliffs between Wisemans Bridge and Amroth. © A.S.T.L.

Examination of the sea cliffs from the lofty vantage point of the old cliff road reveals that these are high and dangerous, being composed of loose, rust-brown shale, often heavily overgrown with brambles and stunted scrub. The first two iron patches (see Kilgetty Ironworks p.44), show up as great open slashes in the line of the cliffs, reaching the edge of the path itself and tumbling unevenly several hundred feet to the beach below. It is now easy to comprehend how many thousands of tons of ore were quarried from these unlikely sites, and how hard and hazardous the work must have been.

Approaching the caravans at Meadow House, the views back across Saundersfoot Bay to Monkstone Point open out dramatically. The edge of the cliff recedes from the path and the intervening area consists of stunted gorse and bracken, and here and there open areas of grass which angle down to the cliff face below. A perfect spot for a picnic or just to lie back in the summer sun and drink in the scenery. Caldey Island now occupies the south-western horizon, and St. Catherine's Island, off Tenby, with its flat-topped fort comes into view behind Monkstone Point. Abreast of the caravan park the seaward hedge largely disappears and reveals an expanse of hummocky grass, rich in

butterflies and cliff-top flowers.

A few hundred yards on, the path turns inland, climbs a few wooden-boarded steps and skirts a vertical shale face from where huge amounts of rock have been torn from the cliffs below. This is Crickdam, one of the largest of the old iron "patches". In its heyday it was provided with workshops, store-houses and a blacksmith's shop. There were also one or two cottages on the cliff, but these have long since crumbled away, although small fragments of the "smithy" still remain on the rocks below.

Approaching Amroth, the coast path leaves the route of the old cliff road by crossing a wooden style into a grassy cliff-top meadow. Through the pines ahead there are extensive views over Amroth village and beach, and on to the cliffs at Telpyn. Plenty of space for the children to let off steam while mum and dad get down to some serious relaxing. Before descending to Amroth, locate the iron gate in the hedge, some 150 yards east of the wooden style. These massive iron gate posts were placed there many years ago by a local farmer, John Williams of Tinker's Hill. They came from the original toll-gate on the old turnpike road to Carmarthen, at Kilanow, a few miles away. This belonged to the Tavernspite Turnpike Trust, and for some reason it escaped the attention of the anti-turnpike Rebecca Rioters who were active in West Wales between 1839-1844.

The cliff path finally drops quickly through the pine trees and bracken to Amroth village. Here you can enjoy a drink and snack in one of the friendly village pubs or cafes, or simply sit on the sea-wall enjoying an ice-cream. The final steep descent to Amroth can be avoided by rejoining the Cliff Road, through the old Turnpike Gateposts and following its more gentle gradient to the main road at Steps Quarry. Turn right down the hill for 300 yards to the village, but watch the traffic, this is a busy road in summer. This alternative route is more relevant to those undertaking this walk in the opposite direction, to "work the tides". The climb up the path to the pine trees could prove a "slog" for less enthusiastic walkers.

When tide conditions allow, locate the section of ancient rusted iron pipe which protrudes from the sand in the corner of the beach in front of the Temple Bar Inn. This is the end of an ADIT, or drainage pipe, laid to remove troublesome water from one of the old inland collieries over 1.5 miles away. Storms have long since broken this pipe away from its original outlet in the foot of the sea-cliffs some yards to the West. Many of the mysterious "wet" patches on the wide beaches of Amroth, Wiseman's Bridge and Saundersfoot are caused by fresh water draining out from old mine workings inland through these Adits, the outlets of which are now completely buried.

On your walk back across the beach locate: a) the coal pillar at the base of the cliff, near the old Burrows patch. Here is an example of the old "pillar and stall" method used for mining coal in Pembrokeshire in the 19th century. This consisted of working parts of a seam by means of "stalls" in between pillars of coal left to support the roof; b) a little to the west of Crickdam, the entrance to a small stone tunnel at the foot of the cliffs. The exact purpose and route of this tunnel is the subject of much local debate. It may have been used to convey trams of iron ore under the cliffs to Wiseman's Bridge where it possibly emerged from the steep bank in the caravan park belonging to the Wiseman's Bridge Inn, known locally as the "corses". A more likely explanation is that it was used to gain access to one or more of the richer deposits of iron ore which could not be reached in any other way. This tunnel was clearly visible in January, 1991, but may well disappear again from time to time as cliff falls and the effects of large storm tides obstruct the entrance with rock debris. Exercise great care at the foot of the cliffs, rocks above are loose and unstable and falls are very common. If you find the tunnel, in the interests of safety do not enter in any circumstances; c) at the Amroth end of the beach you will often find patches of the old sunken forest exposed. However, constantly changing tidal effects on the beach,

which can shift thousands of tons of sand after one storm, make exposure and location a matter of chance. Trees are usually oak, elder and willow, which grew along the shore over 4,000 years ago.

As you make your way back along the clean, wrinkled sand of this fine beach, backed by a tangle of rocky outcrops and barnacle encrusted boulders, try to imagine the scene only 130 years ago. Between 100-200 miners, wielding assorted picks, shovels and crowbars, working in pairs to extract the iron-bearing rock from the cliff face above. Picking out the iron mine (ore), the waste rock and shale would then be despatched to the beach below using the simplest method possible. Sometimes this may have been a chute or a basic wooden scaffolding framework carrying a small trackway along which wheeled tubs conveyed the spoil to the dumps at the head of the beach. Wheelbarrows were often used. This debris was then left for the tide to dispose of, usually along the coast to the east towards Amroth, with the prevailing current. The beach was, thus, nearly always covered with huge amounts of rock litter which would be picked over by women and children to retrieve any valuable iron ore which had been exposed by the washing action of the tide. When beach conditions allowed, local farmers would drive their horses and carts on to the beach to load the carefully collected piles of iron mine for transport to Kilgetty Ironworks. Before these works opened, and during the shut-down periods of its erratic operation, ore continued to be quarried from the patches. Sturdily built open boats were beached as far up the sands as possible and loaded by men and women carrying bags of ore up a strong plank on one side, across another plank over the "hold" where the bag was tipped, and down a plank on the opposite side. These small vessels transported the ore to a number of neighbouring iron-works, e.g. Pembrey and, later, to Port Talbot. In 1876, around the time when

Remains of the Smithy below Crickdam. © A.S.T.L.

137

mining on the patches ceased, iron ore was yielding 9/6d per ton, a little under 50p! If only these cliffs could talk what tales they would have to tell. Tales of a simple life, perhaps of larger-than-life characters, but tales characterised by poverty, squalor, unending grinding physical toil, and constant worry and insecurity.

Make your way back to Wiseman's Bridge and a well-earned drink in the Inn.

CRICKDAM
— By Roscoe Howells

For those who wish to delve further into the social history of this fascinating aspect of South Pembrokeshire's recent past the novel Crickdam by local author Roscoe Howells is a must. This compelling story is set against the troubled background of the local iron industry in the 19th century, exposes the desparate conditions of the miners and their families, and paints a vivid — but authentic — picture of a brutal way of life that has now gone for ever.

Available from all good bookshops in West Wales.

Coal Pillar at base of cliff near Amroth. © A.S.T.L.

Entrance to Tunnel at Crickdam.　　© A.S.T.L.

3. A Circular Walk through the Industrial History of South Pembrokeshire. Wiseman's Bridge — Pleasant Valley — Kilgetty Ironworks — Grove Colliery — Wiseman's Bridge (2.5 miles)

If necessary, use your map to find Wiseman's Bridge, just a mile or two to the East of Saundersfoot. From Wiseman's Bridge Inn walk westwards, back towards Saundersfoot, with the wide beach and high bank of boulders and pebbles on your left. Locate the ruined, ivy-covered stub of a building on your right, forming part of the wall of the beachside caravan park. This is the ruin of the old "Talley House." Here the loads of coal being transported from local mines and surface workings were counted before they were taken onto the beach for loading into open boats, beached here at the top of the tide.

Cross the old stone river bridge and turn sharp right into the shady lane marked by the bus-shelter and telephone kiosk. Notice how straight and level this roadway is compared with the coast road. You are now walking along the route of the old narrow gauge Saundersfoot Railway. This section was built in the 1840s to link the collieries and iron works of Stepaside and Kilgetty, via the coastal tunnels and embankments, to the new harbour at Saundersfoot. Horses were first used to pull the trams of coal. In the 1870s the track was largely relaid with heavier rails, now spiked into wooden sleepers. A sturdy little steam engine was subsequently introduced to pull the small trams of coal. She was named "Rosalind" after the daughter of Charles Ranken Vickerman, the local mine owner and industrialist.

Note the name of the first cottage on your left — "Tramway Cottage." Carry straight on here, off the tarmac road and into the mature woods at the side of the valley, up a very gentle gradient. Towards the end of the 18th Century Lord Milford tried to utilise the stream on your right to construct a canal to transport coal from Stepaside further up the valley, to Wiseman's Bridge, at the mouth, for export from the beach. The project failed, however, and the canal was never completed. The marshy scrub on the valley floor, the clear water of the stream and the extensive woodland on the western side of the valley provide a rich variety of habitats for birds, and numerous species can be identified.

After some distance, the wide trackway swings away from the woods and crosses the stream over an old stone bridge. The overgrown hedges on either side now press in, the path narrows and the ground underfoot is almost black with the remnants of coal dust from the collieries it once served. The final section of the trackway is sandwiched between Heathfield

Court Caravan Park and the stream to your left, and the road down Pleasant Valley at the top of the moss and fern covered bank to your right. It finally emerges onto the road opposite Mill House, with its attendant stream. Turn left up the lane towards Stepaside village. Stop opposite the entrance to the attractive Heathfield Court Caravan Park and locate the arched, brown stone facade of what was once the huge casting shed of the Kilgetty Iron Works (see p.44).

Continue up the lane and locate the last stone cottage on your right, before the road bridge. This, originally, was known as the "Pan and Handle", and it was here on pay night, fortified with local ale, that the quarry workers from nearby Ludchurch and Blaencilgoed would take on the Stepaside colliers in fist fights of legendary ferocity.

Turn left into the Stepaside Industrial Heritage Park. This project has been set up with the support of a variety of government and local authority agencies, and aims to re-awaken public interest in the rich industrial history of the Stepaside, Kilgetty, Wiseman's Bridge and Saundersfoot areas. Unfortunately space does not permit a detailed, step-by-step description of a

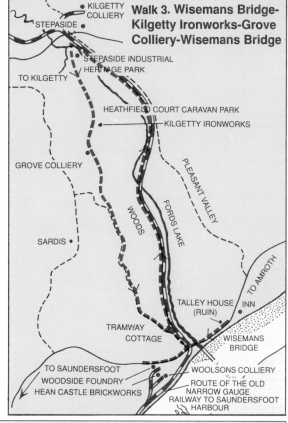

Walk 3. Wisemans Bridge-Kilgetty Ironworks-Grove Colliery-Wisemans Bridge

Kilgetty Ironworks: Workshops, looking South. c. 1865.

139

walk round this extensive site, but I hope the account of the Iron Works together with a visit to the Interpretive Centre (signposted), will enable you to appreciate the significance and scale of this major industrial location. Still clearly visible are the lime kilns, calcining ovens, blacksmith's workshops, loading platform for the blast furnaces, casting shed, now housing the swimming pool for Heathfield Court Caravan Park, engine shed and the site of the blast furnace and its massive stack. Many of these, together with their service trackways which utilised the natural gradient of the steep valley side, are in surprisingly good condition. There is a large picnic area with tables, a duck pond with Mallards and Muscovies, a variety of craft workshops, other exhibits and convenient refreshments.

From the interpretive centre climb the path of the old railway track, past the pond, picnic area and the Ironworks, and make your way up the slope to the woodland clearing housing the old Grove Colliery. The Grove was opened in September, 1856, to supply top quality anthracite coal to the iron works below, and also for export, via the narrow gauge railway to Saundersfoot Harbour. It was one of the deepest mines in South Wales, reaching depths of 640 feet. Underground stabling was provided for 10 pit ponies. The clearing today is still dominated by the powerful tower-like building of the engine house, next to the original shaft which is now covered by a thick concrete slab. Try dropping a small stone through the hole in the middle of the slab and you will be surprised at the time it takes to reach the bottom far below. Other ivy-covered, ruined buildings around the periphery once housed stores, offices,

C. Ranken Vickerman. (Courtesy of Roscoe Howells)

blacksmiths' shops, etc., but now provide shelter only for woodland birds.

Take the footpath out of the opposite side of the clearing, bear to the right up the slope through the woods and emerge onto a small lane. Turn left and follow the narrow lane as it skirts the woods and twists down towards the sea at Wiseman's Bridge. Re-pass "Tramway Cottage" and on reaching the main coast road at the bus shelter, turn right and round the corner to the cream washed houses at the base of the steep hill back towards Saundersfoot. The field opposite, which is now occupied by the Brickyard Caravan Park, was once the site of Woolson's Colliery, Hean Castle Brick Works and Woodside Foundry. This busy little site was serviced by a spur off the Saundersfoot Railway.

The Colliery closed around 1870, having been plagued by drainage problems. The brickworks opened in 1845 and used black clay from the coal bearing strata to manufacture high quality firebricks. The works traded under a variety of names — Thomas Stokes Brick Works 1845, Tenby Silica Co. 1860, Hean Castle Brick Co. 1864, Woolston Firebrick Works 1867! General economic recession caused the works to close in 1887.

Woodside Foundry was established in 1850 to utilise pig iron being produced just up the valley at the Kilgetty Iron Works. Initially it specialised in castings for local collieries and for railways, gas and water works . . . "old brass and iron taken in exchange." After the iron works closed at Stepaside it diversified into marine fittings, domestic ovens, boilers, gates and even cast iron tombstones which are still found in local churchyards, e.g. Sardis, Amroth.

Re-trace your route to the front at Wiseman's Bridge where you can end your walk with a drink and a snack at the comfortable inn, conveniently situated right on the beach.

Grove Pit — remains of the Engine Shed.

4. Tenby-Saundersfoot along the Coast Path (3.75 miles)

A beautiful walk affording some panoramic views of Tenby, Saundersfoot and Carmarthen Bay. However, the terrain is often steeply ridged and the cliffs themselves are of soft shale and must be treated with caution. Remember also to check on transport back to Tenby, if required.

From Tenby, **the start is North Cliff**, then along the old Waterwynch lane, a rather overgrown section leading to **Allen's View**. From here enjoy the almost aerial views of Tenby and the North Bay, over St. Catherine's Island to Caldey and the Caldey Roads in the distance. The path now meanders slightly inland and then descends into the narrow valley which leads to **Waterwynch Cove** (this section of the path may be muddy in wet weather). ★ From Waterwynch the path returns to the cliff edge and winds through bracken (with masses of foxgloves in the early summer), to drop into the pines of **Lodge Valley** where a small waterfall splashes to the beach. The path now passes close to the **Coastguard look-out** perched near to the cliff edge on one of the highest sections of the cliff. From here magnificent views extend to Gower (16.5 miles) and on a clear day to Exmoor (52 miles) and Lundy Island (33 miles). At **Trevayne** the path rises high above Monkstone Beach (p. 58), access by footpath only. After Monkstone the path swings away to the north hugging the cliff edge overlooking **Saundersfoot Bay** and the **Glen Beach**. The final stretch of this walk is through wooded cliffs, bisected by steep shady valleys. The approach to Saundersfoot is made along the beach from the Glen Woods, or at high tide via the road to St. Bride's Hill.

★ For those not able to manage the complete walk, a pleasant alternative is to return from Waterwynch via (a) the lane to the A478, (b) then turn left immediately into the 'Old Road' past Brynhir and thus down a quiet leafy lane to Tenby. (See map).

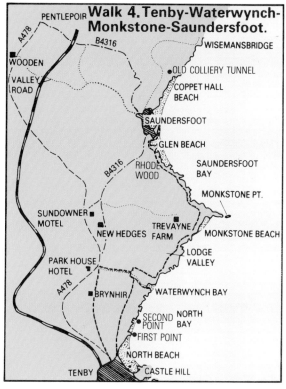

5. Penally-Giltar-Lydstep-Ridgeway-Penally (Circular walk 4.5 miles)

INFORMATION

Part of this walk is through an Army Firing Range at Penally and is liable to be closed to the public. Times of firing are published in local press and warning red flags are flown from prominent spots.

Leave the car park adjacent to the **Penally By-Pass** (A4139) and take the footpath across the railway line and through the **Golf Course** leading to the **South Beach**. Follow the footpath to the top of **Giltar Point**. From here enjoy the marvellous views in all directions — to Caldey and St. Margaret's, back along the length of the South Beach to Tenby and St. Catherine's Island. Lydstep Haven, Manorbier and St. Govan's Head stretch away to the west, while inland the patchwork of farmland fades into the Preseli Hills on the northern horizon. Easy walking now on springy clifftop turf with the sea below washing against the deeply fretted limestone cliffs. The highest point of the cliffs is **Proud Giltar** (exercise care with the nearby blowholes). Shortly after passing this you enter the private estate of **Lydstep Haven Holidays**. Locate the service road through the estate, turn right and return to the entrance with its old lodge cottage. At this point less energetic walkers can return to Penally direct, along the A4139 (1.5 miles). In the summer months a reasonable bus service is available from the estate entrance to Penally.

Those undertaking the complete walk, turn left along the A4139 before turning first right off a sharp bend into a quiet and largely traffic free lane. This lane, which is thick with

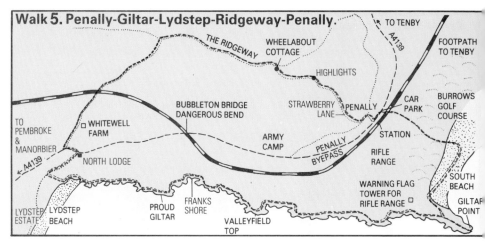

Walk 5. Penally-Giltar-Lydstep-Ridgeway-Penally.

TO TENBY

THE RIDGEWAY

WHEELABOUT COTTAGE

FOOTPATH TO TENBY

HIGHLIGHTS

BUBBLETON BRIDGE
DANGEROUS BEND

STRAWBERRY LANE

PENALLY

CAR PARK

BURROWS GOLF COURSE

TO PEMBROKE & MANORBIER

WHITEWELL FARM

ARMY CAMP

PENALLY BYEPASS

STATION

A4139

NORTH LODGE

RIFLE RANGE

SOUTH BEACH

WARNING FLAG TOWER FOR RIFLE RANGE

GILTAR POINT

LYDSTEP ESTATE

LYDSTEP BEACH

PROUD GILTAR

FRANKS SHORE

VALLEYFIELD TOP

primroses in the early spring, meanders through prime early potato **farmland** and after the railway bridge begins the considerable climb towards the striking escarpment called "The Ridgeway." On joining the Ridgeway, a name which becomes immediately self explanatory, turn right (east), back towards Tenby. To the north are the lower marshy reaches of the **Ritec Valley**, nearly 300 feet below, with **Gumfreston Church** compact and grey on the opposite side of the valley. In the distance the Preseli Hills from the blue-grey horizon. Falling away to the south, the rich red soil in the fields gives way to turf and sheep on the clifftops at Giltar, our route earlier, when perhaps our stride was a little more purposeful than it is now! The familiar landmarks of Caldey and St. Margaret's can be seen across the Caldey Roads, usually with a necklace of small boats and sometimes Lundy Island and the north coast of Devon stand out on

View over Giltar Point towards Caldey Island from Strawberry Lane, Penally.   © A.S.T.L.

Walk 6. Manorbier-Swanlake-Manorbier

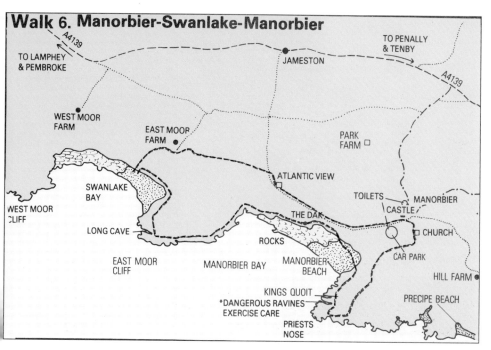

the horizon. At the end of the Ridgeway, turn right at the **"Wheelabout"** (cottage) and follow the lane down to **Penally** and a well earned drink in one of the village pubs.

6. Manorbier-Swanlake Bay-Manorbier (Circular walk 3.75 miles)

Park in the car park just behind **Manorbier Beach** (adjacent to the castle). Turn right at the car park entrance and walk up the hill towards the village. If you have not already visited the **impressive Castle** this is your opportunity. Turn first right and make your way to the small **12th Century Village Church**. Follow the footpath out along the sandstone headland towards the rocky extremity known as the **Priest's Nose**. Stop here to enjoy the glorious coastal views eastward to the old Castle Head and westwards towards Freshwater East and Trewent Point, with St. Govan's Head square and uncompromising at the end of the sequence of bay and rocky headland. Return to Manorbier Beach by the lower path, but exercise care as there are several narrow, extremely deep fissures in the cliffs which extend almost to the footpath. This lower path also passes the **"King's Quoit,"** a Neolithic Burial Chamber (c. 3000 B.C.), with its cap stone of local red sandstone. (This is one of only two such chambers in the whole of the south of the county).

After crossing the beach, make your way along the grassy base of the cliffs, passing the

Manorbier Castle from the South. © A.S.T.L.

'Dak' bungalow overlooking the beach and follow the path as it climbs up the considerable height of the **East Moor Cliff**. Skirt the headland and follow the path to Swanlake Beach (see p. 66), a gorgeous spot to enjoy a snack and a well earned rest, or perhaps a swim. No facilities.

Climb the steep grassy bank behind the beach and make your way to **East Moor Farm**. From here another more direct and level path follows the hedgerows back across the fields to the top of the cliffs west of Manorbier beach. Turn right on entering the lane past lone "Atlantic View" bungalow and descend to the stream in front of the castle (this stream was once diverted and damned to form extensive ponds stocked with fresh fish for the castle!). Now use the footpath back to the car park.

143

Aerial view of Broadhaven Beach.   © *Alan Shepherd Transparency Library*

Broadhaven-Barafundle and Broadhaven-St. Govan's

From the car park above Broadhaven Beach, glorious clifftop walks extend for miles in both directions. Bear in mind, however, that unless you make your own arrangements to be picked up at a pre-arranged venue, you will have to make your own way back to the car park. Public transport in this area is effectively non-existent, so don't be too ambitious.

7. Broadhaven-Barafundle-Broadhaven (Coast Path 3.75 miles)

Set out across the fine sand of **Broadhaven**, with the impressive pinnacle of **Church Rock** just offshore; climb the footpath up the cliffs on the eastern side of the beach, above **Saddle Point**. Here is a magnificent area of dunes and fine sand blown by the prevailing westerlies high above the beach — a rich area for rabbits. Superb walking over level springy turf with excellent coastal scenery, tempting little low water coves, caves and rocks, pounded into fascinating shapes by the unceasing attention of the sea. You will find at least four blowholes, in different stages of development. In the winter gales, air, water and even stones are forced through these with frightening force. The large jutting headland which curves away to the east is **Stackpole Head** — note the lovely, but inaccessible little beach below — **Gun Cliff**. This craggy limestone headland is the home of a colony

of fulmars, and it is also used by **experienced rock climbers**. The various faces have evocative names — Gargoyle Grove, The Hawk, Leaning Tower, The Chimney. From the Point are extensive views towards Caldey and St. Margaret's. Rounding the headland the coastpath skirts the open area of **Stackpole Warren**, before dropping through a rather "stunted" wood to the shelter of **Barafundle Beach**. The final section of this walk is most noticeable for the views it affords of large colonies of sea birds on the cliffs below. The colonies of kittiwakes, guillemots and razorbills are **probably the largest congregation of breeding sea birds on the mainland coast of Pembrokeshire**. Gulls and fulmars breed all along this section of coast from Broadhaven to Barafundle and "choughs" may often be seen feeding on the rough clifftop grass. Also keep a look-out for the **natural cliff arches** and the rather interesting **Griffiths Lort's Hole** in the final section of the cliffs before the descent to the beach.

8. Broadhaven-St. Govan's-Broadhaven (Coast Path 2.5 miles)

Most of this walk lies within the M.O.D. range area, so either check on firing times at Bosherston Post Office, or be prepared to change your route if the range is closed.

From the car park at Broadhaven head off across the clifftops to the south west, often into a

144

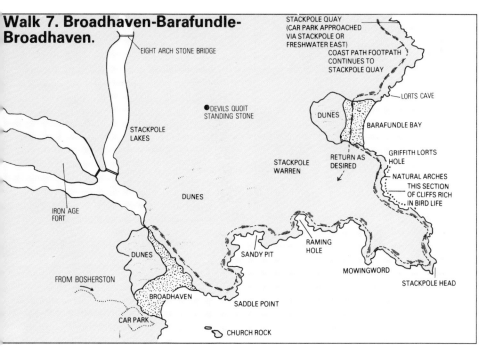

Walk 7. Broadhaven-Barafundle-Broadhaven.

STACKPOLE QUAY
(CAR PARK APPROACHED
VIA STACKPOLE OR
FRESHWATER EAST)

EIGHT ARCH STONE BRIDGE

COAST PATH FOOTPATH
CONTINUES TO
STACKPOLE QUAY

LORTS CAVE

●DEVILS QUOIT
STANDING STONE

DUNES

BARAFUNDLE BAY

STACKPOLE
LAKES

GRIFFITH LORTS
HOLE

STACKPOLE
WARREN

RETURN AS
DESIRED

NATURAL ARCHES

THIS SECTION
OF CLIFFS RICH
IN BIRD LIFE

DUNES

IRON AGE
FORT

DUNES

SANDY PIT

RAMING
HOLE

MOWINGWORD

FROM BOSHERSTON

STACKPOLE HEAD

BROADHAVEN

SADDLE POINT

CAR PARK

CHURCH ROCK

stiff salty breeze straight from the Atlantic, towards the truncated slab of **St. Govan's Head**. Beautiful wild fretted limestone cliffs, pierced by wave battered caves and the occasional tiny low water cove with an apron of sand. Enter the Range area, cross **Trevallen Down** and swing seawards out onto St. Govan's Head. The small inlet at the eastern side of the neck of St. Govan's

Head was used as a **small harbour for Bosherston** and it was here that the tanks for the Castlemartin ranges were once landed and then driven to the range. This little inlet is called Newquay. The short stretch of cliffs to the east, with its stacks and coves, is the home of housemartins, fulmars, shags and razorbills. On the headland the coastguard look-out station

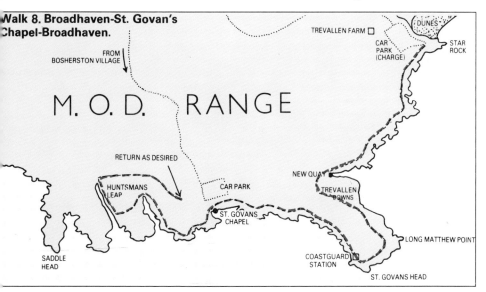

Walk 8. Broadhaven-St. Govan's Chapel-Broadhaven.

TREVALLEN FARM

DUNES

CAR
PARK
(CHARGE)

STAR
ROCK

FROM
BOSHERSTON VILLAGE

M. O. D. RANGE

RETURN AS DESIRED

NEW QUAY

HUNTSMANS
LEAP

CAR PARK

TREVALLEN
DOWNS

ST. GOVANS
CHAPEL

LONG MATTHEW POINT

SADDLE
HEAD

COASTGUARD
STATION

ST. GOVANS HEAD

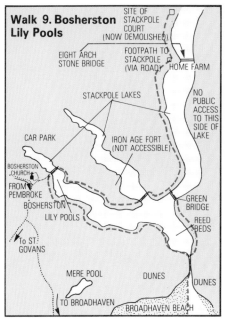

SITE OF STACKPOLE COURT (NOW DEMOLISHED)

EIGHT ARCH STONE BRIDGE

FOOTPATH TO STACKPOLE (VIA ROAD)

HOME FARM

STACKPOLE LAKES

NO PUBLIC ACCESS TO THIS SIDE OF LAKE

CAR PARK

IRON AGE FORT (NOT ACCESSIBLE)

BOSHERSTON CHURCH

FROM PEMBROKE

BOSHERSTON

LILY POOLS

GREEN BRIDGE

REED BEDS

To ST GOVANS

MERE POOL

DUNES

DUNES

TO BROADHAVEN

BROADHAVEN BEACH

perches high above the sheer cliffs, facing westwards along some of the wildest but most majestic cliff scenery in Britain. Sheer grey cliffs with caves and sea carved fissures extend into the distance, while in some bays immense boulders, the

size of houses, absorb and deflect the rolling surf. Huddled against the cliffs, its limestone blocks merging into them, is our destination — **St. Govan's Chaple** (see p. 70). Huntsman's Leap is some 600 yards west and well worth looking at.

9. Bosherston-Lily Pools-Broadhaven- Bosherston (Circular Walk)

Park in the car park next to the parish church of St. Michael, and follow the footpath to the Lily Pools (see sketch map). the three fingers of the artificially created lakes form the largest expanse of open water in the National Park and are part of the 2,000 acre **Stackpole National Nature Reserve** — owned by the National Trust and administered jointly by the Trust and the Nature Conservancy Council.

The **Lily Pools** are the western arm of the lakes — and I suggest you take the more open and sunny eastern bank first and return along the wooded western bank from Broadhaven beach. On the limestone ridge between the first and second lakes the remains of an Iron Age fort may be detected, although this is not now accessible. The Lily Pools of the western arm are **at their best in late spring and early summer** when they present a quite unforgettable sight framed by the clear blue of a May sky. All of the lakes are rich in wildlife, with swans, coot, many species of duck, kingfishers and the tall, stately, ever patient heron. The clear lime-rich waters offer fine coarse fishing, with tench, roach and fine specimens of pike to be

Cliffs at St. Govan's Head. (Note the Coastguard Station in the distance).   © *Alan Shepherd Transparency Library*

146

Bosherston Lily Pools.   © *Alan Shepherd Transparency Library.*

hooked. The eastern lake also has a small otter population. Take care crossing the first and second causeways between the lakes, as they are narrow and unfenced on one side. On reaching the **Green Bridge** you have two options: either (1) continue south past the reed beds and the fringe of **Stackpole Warren** to follow the water escaping from the lake down the rocky culvert to **Broadhaven Beach**; or (2) continue along the western side of the third lake for nearly one mile, skirt the **"Home Farm,"** and the finely proportioned **8-arch stone bridge** to the site of the old Cawdor mansion **"Stackpole Court,"** now sadly demolished and cleared away. However, you can still climb the wide flight of stone steps to the old terrace, high above the lake, and marvel at the gorgeous views which unfold. Sit quietly and let your imagination recreate the lifestyle which went with the beauty of the location — a house with over 300 rooms, some 13,000 acres of land and a staff of 170 employed. On your return to reality make your way back to the Green Bridge and select your route back to the car park at Bosherston. *(* There is no public access across the 8-arch bridge to the eastern bank).*

The walk round the lakes is some 2 miles long and quite level in nature. The excursion up the eastern lake will add approx. 1.5 miles to the total distance covered. On returning to Bosherston village you can rest your legs and enjoy a cup of tea and a home made cake at Mr. and Mrs. Westons "Olde Worlde Tea Rooms."

10. West Angle Bay — Victorian Forts — Super Tankers — Lifeboat Station — Angle Bay and Village – West Angle Bay (A level, circular walk of approx. 3.5 miles)

If necessary use your map to drive to the coastal village of Angle, near to the western tip of South Pembrokeshire, some 8 miles from Pembroke. On arriving at the village via the B4320, turn left following the sign for West Angle Bay. West Angle Bay is an attractive sandy beach, almost at the mouth of the huge Milford Haven Waterway. Just above the beach is a grassy picnic area with testle tables.

Set off over the wooden stile in the right hand corner of the car park, past the old lime kiln. Follow the well marked path along the edge of the low cliffs and out onto the promontory with the old fort of Thorn Island on the rocky islet just offshore. The path runs outside a sheep fence for some distance and the coves below are usually strewn with interesting flotsam and jetsam, bits of fishing nets, driftwood of all shapes and sizes, the occasional battered buoy, and the much more common plastic debris of all sorts. Approaching the fort, which is now a hotel, note that the landing stage is actually a sunken barge. The first plan for a defensive structure on Thorn Island was put forward during the reign of Elizabeth I in 1595. It was not until several hundred years later that an appraisal of the sea

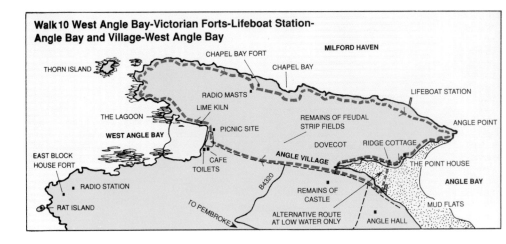

Walk 10 West Angle Bay-Victorian Forts-Lifeboat Station-Angle Bay and Village-West Angle Bay

defences for the new Admiralty Dockyard at Pembroke Dock in 1840 prompted the government to act. Construction of the fort began in 1852 using granite faced blocks, and was completed in the early 1860's. It was converted into a hotel in the 1930's. Behind Thorn Island on the northern shore of the Haven is St. Anne's head, with its lighthouse and coastguard station. West Blockhouse Point, with its huge maritime marker beacons, and the Field Study Centre at Dale Fort are also easily recognisable. The first fort at West Blockhouse was the result of a survey into seaward defences initiated by Sir Thomas Cromwell in 1539. This may have lead on from observations made by Henry VII, who had landed at nearby Mill Bay when he returned from France in 1485. Work on the first fort here, and at East Blockhouse, actually began in 1580. East Blockhouse is marked by the radio masts on the headland to the south of West Angle Bay.

Swinging round to the right, the rocks beneath us change quite suddenly to old red sandstone. The wind appears to tuck in more comfortably behind us, and seems to drop several knots, while the view of the Haven unfolds most dramatically. The fine, sheltered anchorage of Dale Roads opposite leads the eye north, and then, inevitably, east, to expose the vast scale of this mighty waterway. Tankers are usually moored in the waters off St. Ishmaels to the north, while looking up the Haven, the circular fort at Stock Rock is now overshadowed by the sinewy metal jetty thrusting out behind it. This jetty services the Elf Oil Refinery a little inland at Robeston West, and stretches out to the deep water channel almost in the middle of the Haven. Although it was first suggested that Stack Rock should be fortified in 1748, the present structure was actually commenced in 1850 and completed

in the 1860's as part of the chain of forts built to protect the dockyard.

Further upstream another network of jetties off the southern shore provide berthing facilities for the massive Texaco Refinery, and its associated plants at Rhoscrowther. The single, massive chimney which rears up almost 700 ft. into the sky behind the refinery is the stack for the Pembroke power station — one of the largest oil-fired stations in Europe. Still further upstream on the northern bank, past the town of Milford Haven and the "Man of War Roads," is the Gulf Oil Refinery at Waterston, near Neyland.

Chunky, no-nonsense tugs needed for berthing the tankers are often moored in pairs at strategic points up and down the waterway. The deep water channel runs close to the Angle shore here so you may have a grandstand view of a huge tanker entering or leaving Britain's premier oil port.

The path now heads due east, the low seaward cliffs become a steep, bracken covered bank, and after passing between high, impenetrable banks of scrub and gorse which blot out the view on both sides, we arrive at the foot of a high radio mast. Entrance to the compound is strictly forbidden. "Danger of Death. Keep Out." Our views are now reversed. The Haven is obscured behind a narrow belt of wind blown woodland, while Angle village and its rich surrounding farmland claims out attention. This is a noted early potato growing corner of South Pembrokeshire. Many of the narrow fields traversed on this walk are thought to be remnants of the original Norman strip fields.

The path skirts round the ancient Chapel Bay Fort, built as part of further improvements to the haven defences, as a result of a "Report to Parliament on the Sea Defences of Milford Haven and Pembroke Dock," made by a

148

committee appointed by the Secretary of State for War in 1858. It was completed around 1868 but was later modified during the early years of this century as an open battery for heavy guns. A few hundred yards past the two Chapel Bay cottages the path resumes its original route, past an attractive wooded area where oak, beech and ash reach to the water's edge, and the grassy slopes will tempt the less energetic to pause for a while. Past the trees the path emerges onto open farmland of small fields, and crosses a series of wooden stiles before gradually dropping down to meet the service road for the R.N.L.I. lifeboat station. The crew of the Angle Lifeboat cover a particularly wild stretch of the Pembrokeshire Coast, where strong tidal currents aggravate the exposed sea conditions. The lifeboathouse is open to the public. Cross the gravelled car park, and one further wooden stile leads through high banks of gorse and thorn to Angle Point. Opposite is Sawdern Point, with Popton Fort, square and low, let into the hillside on the left. Popton was built as a result of the 1858 Report to Parliament already mentioned, and was completed in 1867. Rounding the point, with its shell of the former lifeboathouse, the wide expanse of Angle Bay becomes apparent, its size perhaps accentuated by the uniform lowness of its surroundings. This huge, shallow bay, sheltered from the prevailing westerly winds, makes an excellent anchorage for small boats. It once sustained rich cockle beds on the muddy shore at Kilpaison opposite, but these largely disappeared with the arrival of the oil industry.

The shallow waters of the muddy foreshore echo the plaintive call of the curlew, while waders, ducks, gulls, herons and, further out into the bay, cormorants, are frequent visitors. Ahead the "Old Point House Inn" makes a convenient spot to stop for a drink. If it is warm sit at one of the outside tables above the foreshore clutter of lobster pots, beached boats and general maritime bric-a-brac. The piles of seaweed along the shingle beach ensure that the air has a suitably salty tang. Follow the rutted roadway along the shore for several hundred yards and locate "Ridge Cottage" and "Snug Harbour" on your right. At extreme low water it is possible to cross the creek here. Walk to the end of the shingle spur, then across a concrete slab let into the mud at the low part of the channel, and make for the opposite shore in line with the two red brick pillars marking the gap in the low wall, leaving the derelict old quay on your left. If the tide is in, continue on the roadway round the edge of the creek until you re-join the main street through the village. Turn right past St. Mary's Church and the village school. Behind the houses on the left locate the last remnants of Angle Castle. Next to the school is a neat little public garden, with a collection of variegated shrubs clustering round a sombre memorial. This was erected by the "Tenantry" to John Mirehouse, their "much beloved and respected landlord," who died in 1864. The Mirehouse family still live in Angle Hall on the outskirts of the village, and remain the major local landowner. This pleasant little village only has one street, and it is an interesting architectural melange of old and new — cottages, bungalows and houses with salmon pink and delicate primrose yellow most often used for outside elevations. It has a quiet, self-contained feel about it. Lobster pots and bits of fishing nets mingle happily with potatoes and beans in the gardens. The colonaded Globe Hotel, and the neighbouring Hibernian Inn provide focal points for the village social life. Make your way back to West Angle Bay where Mr. and Mrs. Williams will be happy to welcome you into their beachside cafe for refreshments.

Oil Jetties at Popton Fort with East Angle Bay behind.   © *Alan Shepherd Transparency Library*

149

Gardens to Visit

Picton Castle Gardens — early Spring.   © *Alan Shepherd Transparency Library*

Picton Castle

Picton Castle was built around 1190 by William de Picton, a Norman knight who came to West Wales with Arnulf de Montgomery, one of the builders of the great fortress at Pembroke. The present owners, the Hon. R. Hanning and Lady Màrion Philipps can trace their ancestors in direct line for 800 years to the original founder. Throughout the centuries the family has provided many prominent public spirited people to the counties of Pembroke, Carmarthen and Cardigan, e.g. 52 High Sheriffs, 25 Members of Parliament, Lord Lieutenants and many Magistrates. The Hon. R. Philipps is the present Lord Lieutenant of Dyfed.

Since moving into the Castle in 1954 the present owners have transformed the gardens. By using and enhancing the natural beauty of the site and by carefully providing shelter for a huge assortment of trees, shrubs and plants, which have been collected from all over the world, beautiful gardens have been created, which provide colour and form throughout the year. Rhododendrons flower from February to July; Camellias from February to May; Magnolias from spring to summer. In April the gardens are ablaze with the colour of flowering trees —

cherries, crab apples, etc. — while in June and July the Liquid Amber Tree, Leptosternum and the bottle brush shrubs from Australia add an exotic note to these tranquil surroundings. The warm days of mid-summer belong to the blue Aganpanthus and pink and white Crinum and Arum Lillies from South Africa, the varieties of Eurcyphias and pink and red Escallonias.

The ancient oaks, evergreens and flowering trees and shrubs of these extensive gardens near to the estuary of the Eastern Cleddau form a rich habitat for wildlife. Treecreepers, nuthatches, woodpeckers, tits, flycatchers, warblers and many other species occur in numbers.

* Location, opening times, etc., — refer to relevant advertisement (above).

Upton Castle Grounds

Location: At **Milton** on the main A477 Tenby to Pembroke Dock road, turn in past the ivy covered **Milton Brewery**. Follow this narrow lane for a little over 2 miles, past the entrance for Paskeston Lodge, before bearing right at the next fork. After 600 yards pass the small lodge cottage and enter the tree lined castle drive.

The castle was originally one of the

smaller outposts of Pembroke Castle, and overlooks the Carew River. The grounds have been open to the public since 1976, when the National Park took over the responsibility for a large part of the woodland garden and the terraces. The castle and the lawns immediately adjacent to the house are private. Visitors are recommended to study the map in the car park before setting off to view these lovely gardens. Most of the paths through the garden are quite sound, but after wet weather sensible walking shoes are advisable.

The grounds, which extend to over thirty acres, contain over 250 species of mature trees and shrubs, many of which are labelled. In particular there are many magnificent specimens of rhododendrons, camellias and magnolias. Three elevated terraces, complete with extensive rose beds, a delightful summer house and goldfish ponds provide a wonderful setting for a stroll in the afternoon sun. A free car park is provided and there are adjacent toilets. Upton Castle grounds are open to the public from 10am-4.30pm every Tues., Wed., Thurs., Fri., between February and October (inclusive). They are also open on Spring and Summer Bank Holiday Mondays.

Colby Lodge
The beautiful gardens of Colby Lodge lie in a sheltered, tree-lined valley near the coastal village of Amroth. The property is owned by the National Trust who have undertaken extensive work in clearing, pruning and generally tending the huge variety of specimen trees and shrubs which have been established there over the years. There are refreshments, toilets and a gravelled car park. Gardens are open from 31st March - 3rd November each year.

Location: From Amroth seafront, turn at either the Amroth Arms or at Amroth Castle. (These two narrow lanes merge at Amroth School). Continue past the school for 100 yards, turn left and after half mile locate Colby Lodge on your left.

Rhododendrons and Azaleas glow with colour. Picton Castle Gardens. © A.S.T.L.

151

Holiday Services

This next section of the Guide is designed to answer most of the "where can I find?" questions asked by many visitors to South Pembrokeshire each year. I hope this will allow you to use as much of your hard earned holiday time enjoying yourself and not wasting time searching for services in a strange area.

Taxi Services

Photography

JIM'S TAXIS

Large fleet – all radio controlled
8 Seater Minibus
Airports, Trains, Buses etc.
Open 7 days a week
Contracts and Accounts welcome
Telephone: Tenby 3678

Squibbs Studios

Pembrokeshire's
Specialists
in
Photography
for over
100 Years

FOR ALL YOUR REQUIREMENTS

Cameras - Projectors - Binoculars
Radios - Films - etc.

Professional 24 hour Developing and
Printing Service with
FREE COLOUR £1.99 ENLARGEMENT
at
WARREN STREET, TENBY
Telephone: 2109
and
CAMBRIAN TERRACE, SAUNDERSFOOT

Hairdressers

Christopher & Christine

Vernon House – St. Julian Street
Telephone: Tenby 2445

LADIES' HAIR DESIGN SALON
Specialists in Cutting, Colouring and Perming

GENTLEMAN'S HAIR SALON
Specialists in all aspects of Gents' styling

BEAUTY SALON
with full range of Treatments available.

152

Roys Fish & Chip Shop

UPPER PARK ROAD, TENBY
Tel: (0834) 4240
(Near Multi-Storey Car Park)

Roy and his staff
would like to welcome you
to our spacious self service
restaurant with seating for 68.

We offer a comprehensive selection
of reasonably priced,
sit down family meals
with reductions for children.

Or try a delicious take away meal
from our extensive menu.

Hours of opening:
11.45am–11.00pm

D. Fecci & Sons
FISH & CHIP RESTAURANT
with
FULL TAKE AWAY SERVICE
Lower Frog Street, Tenby
(just 40 yards through the Five Arches)
THE HOME OF FINE FRIED FOODS
Our extensive menu includes: Fish, Curry,
Chicken, Baked Potatoes, Vegetarian,
Tasty Snack Dishes
Children's Menu always available
Reductions for O.A.P.s

GOOD FOOD
FRIENDLY & EFFICIENT SERVICE
REASONABLE PRICES
Featured in the Gourmet Guide
to Fish & Chips
by Pierre Picton & Rod Harrod

Open 7 days a week
Mon-Thurs: 11.30-11.30
Fri & Sat: 11.30-12.00

TAKE AWAY SERVICE
Select your favourite from our huge range of
9" & 12" Regular & Deep Pan Pizza's.
These include Designer, Hula Hula, Tuna,
Tenby Seafood, Vegetarian, American
Porky, Sidewalk and our famous
Ring Stinger.

Sample our mouth watering American Style
Burgers, Hot Dogs, Kebabs and Jacket
Potatoes, Vegetarian take aways.

Fast, friendly service throughout the day
and on 'till late in the evening.
RAPPI'S, UPPER FROG STREET,
TENBY.
TEL: (0834) 4712

TAKE AWAY SANDWICH BAR

Huge selection of
freshly prepared
sandwiches and rolls
with delicious fillings to
suit all tastes. Quick, friendly
service and reasonable prices.

Cold drinks and confectionary

LOCATED NEXT TO ST. MARY'S CHURCH,
TENBY – AT THE TOP OF
CRESSWELL STREET.
TEL: 4252

TOURIST INFORMATION CENTRES

Comprehensive holiday information can be obtained at all of the following centres from friendly and helpful staff.

TENBY South Pembs. District Council and Pembrokeshire Coast National Park. The Information Centre, The Croft, Tenby. Tel: (0834) 2402.

KILGETTY National Parks Information Centre. Tel: (0834) 812175. South Pembrokeshire District Council. Tel: (0834) 813672.

SAUNDERSFOOT National Parks Information Centre, The Harbour. Tel: (0834) 811411.

PEMBROKE Pembrokeshire Coast National Park, The Drill Hall, Castle Terrace, Pembroke. Tel: (0646) 682148.

HAVERFORDWEST Preseli Pembrokeshire District Council, Old Bridge, Haverfordwest. Tel: (0437) 763110.

FISHGUARD Preseli Pembrokeshire District Council, Hamilton Street, Fishguard. Tel: (0348) 873484.

BROADHAVEN (North) Pembrokeshire Coast National Park, Countryside Unit, Broadhaven. Tel: (0437) 781412.

ST. DAVID'S Pembrokeshire Coast National Park Information Centre, City Hall. Tel: (0437) 720392.

NEWPORT (Dyfed) Pembrokeshire Coast National Park Information Centre, Carningli Centre. Tel: (0239) 820912.

MILFORD HAVEN Preseli Pembrokeshire District Council Information Cenre, The Town Hall, Hamilton Terrace, Milford Haven. Tel: (0646) 692501.

Most of the above information centres are open from around Easter-October each year. Enquiries for information at all other times should be made to:

South Pembs. District Council, Information Centre, Tenby. (Details above).

Information Officer, Pembrokeshire Coast National Park, County Offices, Haverfordwest. Tel (0437) 764591.

Tourist Information Dept., Preseli Pembrokeshire District Council, Cambria House, Haverfordwest. Tel: (0437) 766774.

In the Evening

Sunset, Tenby Harbour.   © A.S.T.L.

When the sun finally goes down, and the last stragglers have reluctantly dragged themselves away from the beaches, a whole new facet of South Pembrokeshire comes to life. For those who can summon up the energy there is plenty to do — go to one of the Donkey Derbies, take the family to see Auto Grass Racing, or for a restful cruise along the coast passing the quiet and now shady beaches. Enjoy a display by the Tenby Lifeboat and the Air Sea Rescue Helicopter in North Bay, or a Raft Race for charity from the natural grandstand of the North Walk. Visit one of the events organised within the dramatic confines of Pembroke Castle, or thrill to the harmony of a major Welsh Male Voice Choir in St. Mary's Church. Take in a lively show at the De Valence Pavilion, have a game or two of Bingo, play a few frames of snooker, enjoy the easy atmosphere of a Folk Club, and dance into the early hours under the bright lights of a Disco.

You may prefer an easy walk across your favourite beach, or simply to sit and watch the boats return to their moorings as the harbourside lights come on in Tenby and Saundersfoot. The attractive bustle of the various shops in Tenby, Saundersfoot and Pembroke, which stay open late in the evening, may claim your attention, before you slip into one of the many cosy pubs to taste the local Welsh brew.

Let's have a Drink and a Meal out

If a hard day's sunbathing at Barafundle, or your windsurfing lesson on the beach at Saundersfoot have left you thirsty and dry, a look through these next pages will bring you instant relief! South Pembrokeshire will allow you plenty of scope to enjoy your favourite "sundowner" and to experiment with new ones, but watch those local brews — they pack quite a punch. Here you will find a wide variety of pubs, inns and restaurants in which to end that perfect day out. Many are old and picturesque, some have spectacular views over sea and estuary, others re-create a period atmosphere and have a special charm and personality, while others have worked hard to build up an enviable reputation for good food, choice wines or real ale. Lots of pubs welcome families and many have well equipped children's rooms. Some of the larger inns and hotel bars organise live entertainment for their summer visitors. Those holidaymakers on a restricted budget can enjoy an inexpensive meal in one of the cafés catering for families, or you can pamper yourself by dining in three star elegance at one of the sophisticated clifftop restaurants. The choice is yours — enjoy yourselves. Use the Good Eating and Drinking Guide overleaf to help you plan your evening, but remember the drink/drive laws and if necessary use one of the local taxi services to ensure that your holiday evening does not end on a sour note. (Taxi information, p. 152).

EVENING ENTERTAINMENT

Details are given on page 167. In addition, remember that many of the local hotels, larger bars and country inns organise a variety of live entertainment nightly. The Tenby Information Centre may have additional information, but also keep your eyes open for local advertising posters, etc.

St. Margaret's Fair

At one time a major event in the social life of Tenby and the surrounding community — it dates from a Charter granted by Elizabeth I. It is usually held in the middle of July, from Wed. noon-Sat. evening. The opening ceremony is a colourful spectacle with the Mayor, Town Crier and Town Band in procession. Of late the number of traditional fairground amusements have declined and have been replaced by a variety of market stalls.

Bingo

Warren Social Club, Warren Street, Tenby.
British Legion Club, Lower Frog Street, Tenby.
Conservative Club, St. Florence Parade, Tenby.
The Ex-Servicemen's Club, South Parade, Tenby.
De Valence Pavilion, Upper Frog Street, Tenby.

Good Eating and Drinking Guide

This section is organised on an East-West progression across South Pembrokeshire and presents recommended pubs and restaurants from Amroth in the East to Pembroke in the West. Wherever you are staying or happen to find yourself after a day's exploring, this Guide will help you to round off your day, enjoying good food and drink in pleasant and friendly surroundings.

Eating out in Amroth

158

Woodridge Inn
and Squash Club

WOODEN, Nr. SAUNDERSFOOT

This large Family Pub is situated on the main A487 road into Tenby. We are open from 9.00 a.m. to 11..00 p.m. and offer a wide selection of delicious Bar Meals throughout the day.

★ In addition to the squash courts it also offers a gymnasium, sauna, solarium and full sized snooker table.
★ Life entertainment most evenings.
★ Burton and local Pembrokeshire Ales
★ Large Car Park
★ Children's play area adjacent to the terrace

Under the personal supervision of the Owners Mr. and Mrs. Dibble.

Telephone: Saundersfoot (0834) 812259

The Ashburnham Arms

KILGETTY, Nr SAUNDERSFOOT
(On the main A478 Carmarthen-Tenby Road).

Tel: (0834) 811750

☆ Bar meals all day, every day
☆ Live music every Saturday
☆ Children's play area
☆ Traditional Sunday lunch
☆ Bed/breakfast all year
☆ Large Car Park

COEDMOR RESTAURANT
Amroth

A family run restaurant with Olde Worlde charm, on the edge of the sea at Amroth. Whatever the time of day we'll be delighted to serve you.

We open early for morning coffee, followed by our special menu, changed daily, or choose from our A la Carte Menu.

Call in with your family for Sunday lunch or admire the view while enjoying a delicious cream tea. We are always open & you are assured of excellent food, a friendly atmosphere and sensible prices.

For evening & Sunday bookings
Tel: (0834) 813915

The Cavalier Restaurant

High Street, Saundersfoot

Near the Harbour Car Park & just 3 minutes from the Beach.

Excellent food available throughout the day. Morning Coffee, Lunch, Afternoon Teas and Evening Meals – all at reasonable prices. Traditional Sunday Lunch, Fully Licensed. Children welcome.

All Meals are carefully cooked to order. **Tel: (0834) 812806**

ROYAL OAK INN

WOGANS TERRACE, SAUNDERSFOOT
Tel: (0834) 812546

Set in the heart of the village the Oak is proud of its traditional cooking. Fresh fish from the local quaysides provide the menu's staple dishes: Milford Plaice, Dover & Lemon Sole, Mackerel etc. Daily specials such as Boef Bourguignon & Coq au Vin sharpen the appetite and vegetarian meals are also served. An extensive bar menu is available.

At the bar choose from three real ales, 60 malt whiskies, and a wine list to match.

Open all day for food, conveniently situated only yards from the village beach.

EATING OUT IN TENBY

During the life of this Guide the telephone numbers of the Tenby Exchange will change. All existing 4-figure numbers will be prefixed by 84. The Area Code will remain 0834.

The PARK HOUSE Hotel

Narberth Road, Tenby, Dyfed
Telephone: Tenby 2528 / 3955

This Gourmet Restaurant serving Game, Fresh Local Fish, Lobsters, King Prawns, Veal, Duck Breast, Poultry, Prime Steaks, Salads, fresh produce (mostly from our own farm) is situated adjacent to the luxurious indoor swimming pool in the Park House Hotel Leisure Complex. Other amenities open to diners; Squash, Tennis, Jacuzzi, Sauna & Solariums.

Lunch 12.00 to 2.30 p.m.–Afternoon Teas
Dinner 6.30 to 10 p.m.
· FINE WINES & PORT
Children very welcome. Licensed. Ample parking
Visa & Access accepted

Table reservations TENBY 2528 / 3955

The

Park House Poolside Restaurant
A LA CARTE

NOW AVAILABLE 3 BED LUXURY APARTMENTS FOR SALE ADJOINING LEISURE COMPLEX

Pam Pam
Restaurant
TUDOR SQUARE – TENBY
Telephone: (0834) 2946

A licensed Family Restaurant where children are especially welcome.

Serving:
★ Morning Coffee ★ Lunches
★ Afternoon Teas
★ Evening Meals
★ Live Entertainment

Our goal is to provide you with the best food – attractively presented – at a price which is kind on your pocket and represents real value for money.

Open: 10 a.m. to 10 p.m.

CHARNY'S

The Family Restaurant

HIGH STREET, TENBY
Telephone: TENBY (0834) 2024

Open:
10.00am to 10.00pm

*Meals served all day
Plus Morning Coffee
and Afternoon Teas*

During the life of this Guide the telephone numbers of the Tenby Exchange will change. All existing 4-figure numbers will be prefixed by 84. The Area Code will remain 0834.

FOR SUPERB CUISINE

Chortles is open throughout the day and offers an intimate bistro type atmosphere. In the evening enjoy a sophisticated candlelit dinner – complemented with fine wine from our cellar.

Come and try our huge variety of specialty dishes – which feature the best of local produce – prepared and cooked with care and imagination. Full grill menu. Top value traditional Sunday lunches – vegetarian dishes always available.

Situated right in the heart of the High Street, Tenby – opposite Currys.

TEL: TENBY 2274

Tenby House Hotel
TUDOR SQUARE TENBY

Tenby House is built on the site of The Old Globe Coaching Inn. Between 1805 and 1824 it was the elegant home of Sir William Paxton a London banker, who was largely responsible for the development of the town as a fashionable regency resort.

Today Tenby House remains at the forefront of good food and accommodation. This town centre hotel and free house now offers several lively bars and enjoys an excellent reputation for its real ales and good value bar menu's. Morning and afternoon tea and coffee are available and hot and cold meals are served throughout the day in the bars and in our sunny beer garden. Traditional Sunday lunch is our speciality and a childrens menu is always to hand.

Our well appointed accommodation in en-suite bedrooms will ensure that your holiday is an enjoyable one – and Tenby's beaches and picturesque harbour are only a few minutes walk away. All rooms have tea making facilities, colour T.V. central heating etc., special short break holidays arranged.

WTB
With Merit

Tel: (0834) 2000 & 2868 Fax: (0834) 2868

During the life of this Guide the telephone numbers of the Tenby Exchange will change. All existing 4-figure numbers will be prefixed by 84. The Area Code will remain 0834.

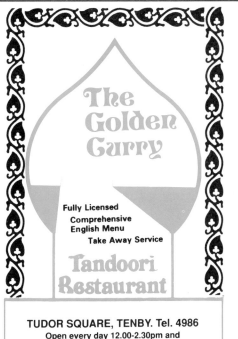

The Golden Curry

Fully Licensed
Comprehensive English Menu
Take Away Service

Tandoori Restaurant

TUDOR SQUARE, TENBY. Tel. 4986
Open every day 12.00-2.30pm and
5.30pm to Midnight (including all holidays)

Normandie Hotel
UPPER FROG STREET, TENBY
Tel: (0834) 2227

The Normandie Hotel is an old coaching inn occupying a central position within the medieval town of Tenby. Main entrance Upper Frog Street – also entry through **The Town Walls** on South Parade. Here you can enjoy a gourmet evening with fine wines and excellent service in the relaxing atmosphere of our "Olde Worlde" restaurant. The extensive range of home cooked bar meals which are available in our suite of 3 bars and family room between 12am & 2pm gained The Normandie a place in Egon Ronay's "Just A Bite" guide. Children catered for. (Bar Meals 7-10pm. Lounge Bar Only). Bed and breakfast accommodation also available.

Under the personal supervision of Chris and Anita Wooles
Access & Visa Accepted

ROYAL Gate House HOTEL

Tenby's premier hotel, provides a high standard of comfort and service. The hotel's 60 bedrooms, many with sea views, all have television, courtesy tray and baby listening service; ensuite rooms also have colour television and telephone. In addition to the two restaurants and four bars, guests are now able to enjoy the facilities of our new, well equipped sports complex.

Sports Complex — Sauna, Solarium, Gymnasium, Steam Tub, Squash, Swimming Pool, Games Room.

The hotel caters for all types of holidays — Bargain Breaks, Mini Weekends, special terms for children.

The ideal hotel for Weddings, Conferences, Seminars and Functions.

The Hotel with something for everyone

North Beach, Tenby, Dyfed SA70 7ET Telephone: Tenby (0834) 2255

RAPPI'S PIZZERIA

Huge range of delicious pizzas to cater for all the families special preferences. 9" & 12" Regular and Deep Pan pizzas available, including Designer, Hula Hula, Tuna, Tenby Seafood, Vegetarian, American Porky, Sidewalk, and our famous Ring Stinger.
OR sample our delicious American Style Burgers, Hot Dogs, Kebabs and Jacket Potatoes, Vegetarian meals always available.

Our range of exotic ice cream sundaes make a great way to complete your meal – or provide an enjoyable break when served alone. Parties of all kinds catered for – please ask for details.

Home Delivery Take Away Service available.
Open all day 'till late in the evening
RAPPI'S, UPPER FROG STREET, TENBY.
TEL: (0834) 4712

EATING OUT
LYDSTEP
MANORBIER
JAMESTON
MILTON

Chives Restaurant and Tea Rooms

Open daily from 10.30 a.m.
Adjacent to Village Stores, Manorbier
Telephone: 871230
Morning Coffee – Lunches – Pembrokeshire Cream Teas – Evening Meals
Enjoy choosing from our extensive à la carte or vegetarian menus.
Come and see us after
visiting the Castle or the beach.
A warm village welcome awaits you
and your family.

St Julians Restaurant/Bistro

1 Bridge Street, Tenby Tel: 4577
(Overlooking Tenby Harbour)
Exclusive Coffee Lounge · Huge Selection of Freshly Cut Sandwiches with delicious fillings to suit all tastes.
Home Made Cakes · Local Seafood dishes · Evening Meals · Extensive Wine List · Children welcome
A Family run Restaurant with a friendly 'Olde Worlde' atmosphere

---

Eating Out — Tenby

FECCI & SONS

ICE CREAM PARLOUR & SNACK BAR
Upper Frog Street, Tenby
OFTEN LICKED
BUT NEVER BETTERED
No visit to Tenby is complete unless you sample one of our huge selection of over 60 speciality ice cream dishes
Our family have been creating mouth watering exotic ices for over 50 years and look forward to serving your special favourite
Tea, Coffee and a variety of freshly prepared snacks
OPEN 7 DAYS A WEEK EARLY TILL LATE

XVIIth CENTURY
SWANLAKE INN JAMESTON
(On the A4139 between Tenby & Pembroke)
Three bars – Beer garden
– Choice of real ales
Children are always welcome in our spacious new family room.
Ample car parking.
Meals from £1.00 – Lunch & Evenings
7 days per week
Tel: (0834) 871262

LYDSTEP TAVERN

A friendly family inn situated on the A4139 coast road between Tenby & Manorbier

All kinds of functions welcome: Weddings, Aniversaries, Christmas parties, etc.

Year round comprehensive menus to suit all tastes & pockets.
Sunday Lunch served
Children welcome
Real ales & fine wine.

Large Car Park.   **Tel: (0834) 871521**

Milton Manor Hotel

MILTON – NR. PEMBROKE

Garden Hotel, situated on its own seven acre grounds on the main Pembroke to Carmarthen road (A477).

Elegant Restaurant
Cream Teas served on the terrace
Morning Coffee
Wide range of Bar Meals
Traditional Sunday Lunch

**Telephone:
Carew (0646) 651398**

Eating Out in Pembroke

Pembroke Unicorn Carvery

THE COMMON, PEMBROKE
Telephone: (0646) 685759 or 686224

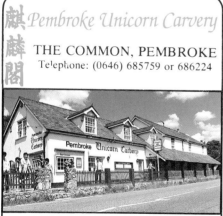

☆ English and Chinese Kitchen
☆ Traditional Sunday Lunch
☆ Licensed Restaurant seating up to 170
☆ Wide selection of Children's Special Menus available
☆ Full Chinese Take Away Service from 5pm-11pm (Mon-Sat) Sun 5pm-9.30pm
☆ Coach Parties welcome
☆ Car Park opposite

Open daily throughout the year including Bank Holidays from 10.30 a.m. – Last orders at 9.30 p.m.

Hollyland Country House Hotel

Set amidst 4 acres of woodland and lawn, the hotel offers peace, comfort and magnificent cuisine. Here is an elegant central base from which to explore the exhilarating scenery of the National Park.
Under the personal supervision of the chef/proprietor the restaurant has an enviable local reputation for the variety and creativity of its menus, the quality of its meals and the professional and courteous service of the staff. Whether you stay with us as a guest in one of our 12 beautifully appointed en-suite bedrooms, or visit us for a sophisticated evening out, we are confident your stay will be enjoyable and we hope you will become one of our many friends who return again and again. Functions and parties, trade shows and business conferences expertly organised by our experienced and willing staff.
We are located just outside Pembroke — on the main A4075 road to Tenby.

Tel: (0646) 681444

EVENING ENTERTAINMENT

TORCH THEATRE
ST. PETER'S ROAD, MILFORD HAVEN
PEMBROKESHIRE, DYFED SA73 2BU

BOX OFFICE: (0646) 695267

West Wales only Repertory Theatre

☆ Drama ☆ Comedy ☆ Classics
☆ Dance ☆ Music ☆ Children's Shows
☆ Visiting Artistes ☆ Film ☆ Licensed Bar

Kiln Park Entertainment Centre, Tenby.

During the life of this Guide the telephone numbers of the Tenby Exchange will change. All existing 4-figure numbers will be prefixed by 84. The Area Code will remain 0834.

DE VALENCE PAVILION – TENBY

The **Entertainment Centre within Tenby's ancient walls.**
Capacity for over 500.
10% Discount for Groups and Parties over 10 persons.

★ Variety Shows

★ Cabaret Nights

★ Dramatic Plays

★ Brass Band Concerts

★ Welsh Male Voice Choirs

★ Family Disco/Dances

★ Conferences

★ Licensed Bars and Café

★ Pre-Booking Facilities

For details of weekly programme
see posters or Telephone: Tenby 2730

COMING BACK NEXT YEAR?

If you have enjoyed your holiday — and I am quite sure you will have done! — you may want to think about booking up for next year before returning home. Why not call into one of the local Estate Agencies for a chat about some possible options, or simply to place your name on their ever-growing mailing lists for a brochure?

You will find the addresses of the main agencies on these two pages.

THINKING OF RETIRING OR MOVING TO PEMBROKESHIRE?

South Pembrokeshire, with its many scenic and climatic advantages, its English speaking heritage and its general quality of life, continues to attract new residents from all over Britain. Many of the local businesses, hotels and guest houses are now owned by people who were born far from this area, but who have assimilated easily into the local community.

If you are thinking of moving and would like professional help and information, the leading Estate Agents operating in the South Pembrokeshire area are found on these pages.

Windsurfing off The Esplanade, Tenby © A.S.T.L.

Self Catering

We offer a choice selection of over 350 holiday cottages, houses, flats and farmhouses in:

TENBY, SAUNDERSFOOT, AMROTH, WISEMANS BRIDGE, PENALLY, MANORBIER

and many other picturesque coastal and country locations.

Free Colour Brochure from:

ST. JULIAN STREET, TENBY
OR DIAL A BROCHURE – TENBY (0834) 2207

During the life of this Guide the telephone numbers of the Tenby Exchange will change. All existing 4-figure numbers will be prefixed by 84. The Area Code will remain 0834.

170

BUY YOUR OWN HOLIDAY HOME
MEADOW HOUSE
HOLIDAY PARK
AMROTH PEMBROKESHIRE

Sited in the beautiful Pembrokeshire Coast National Park overlooking Carmarthen Bay with magnificent views of Worms Head, Pendine Sands, Saundersfoot Bay, Monkstone Point and Caldey Island.

Own your own luxury holiday home on this "Families Only" Holiday Park with its own licensed clubhouse, heated indoor swimming pool, nine pin skittle alley, dance floors and restaurant.

Families are also assured of a warm welcome when they use our well serviced touring caravan & tent park, which provides an ideal base for exploring the National Park.

New and secondhand static caravans may be purchased for private family use by contacting the resident park owners, Mr & Mrs Mel Davies, Meadow House Holiday Park, Amroth, Narberth, Pembrokeshire, SA67 8NS Tel: (0834) 812438.

Caravan Parks — Amroth

Swallow Tree Gardens

Swallow Tree is a small, tranquil, family-run park, set yards from the sea and close to Saundersfoot. It is secluded and beautiful, with superb sea views and lovely grounds. We offer modern, luxurious holiday homes. Three bedroomed, beautifully appointed, pine lodges are available for hire or sale.

Our caravan homes are all fully serviced, many are 12' wide, most are three bedroomed and equipped with microwave, fridge-freezer and duvets.

Our small bar and family restaurant enjoys magnificent sea views, patio and children's play area and good home cooking at reasonable prices.

Ten high-quality touring pitches are also available at Swallow Tree, each with electric hook-up, waste water disposal point and water tap.

TRY SWALLOW TREE GARDENS
SMALL IS BEAUTIFUL,
BUT
SMALL AND BEAUTIFUL IS BEST

DRAGON

AWARD

Free Colour Brochure

SWALLOW TREE GARDENS
Saundersfoot, Pembrokeshire,
Dyfed SA69 9DE
Telephone: (0834) 812398

Caravan Parks — Saundersfoot and Tenby

SALTERN CARAVAN PARK
THE GREEN, TENBY SA70 8EP Tel: 0834 2157

The nearest Holiday Park to Tenby town centre and all main beaches. Within easy walking distance of all the town's main attractions. Small and friendly Park catering for the carefree family holiday. Luxury models with all modern conveniencs. Standard models also available with mains services. Shower and toilet blocks (H & C). Launderette. Ample car parking and only a few minutes' walk from the coach and train stations. Mini breaks and mid week bookings accepted.

SAUNDERSFOOT BAY
—LEISURE PARK—

PRINCE OF WALES AWARD

Caravan Parks — Manorbier

South Wales Premier Holiday Park
☆ **HOLIDAY HOME OWNERSHIP NOW AVAILABLE**

Marsh Road Tenby Dyfed SA70 7RB

Telephone: Bookings & Enquiries	(0834) 4121
Caravan Sales (On-Site)	(0834) 4126
Fax:	(0834) 2437
Caravan Sales (Off-Site)	(0834) 4440
Fax:	(0834) 4541
Social Club	(0834) 3406
Telex	48620 SESIDE G

Caravan Parks — Tenby